Testimonials

A brilliant practical guidebook and psychological kitbag for athletes and coaches written by authors who really get what it's like to be on the frontline of performance, busting unhelpful sports psychology myths and media cliches along the way.

CATH BISHOP, OLYMPIAN, CULTURE COACH AND AUTHOR OF THE LONG WIN

An opportunity for Athletes, Coaches, Parents and anyone else wanting to unlock their full potential, with useful toolkits along the way and help think more clearly through life's obstacles.

KAT RATNAPALA, ENGLAND NETBALL FUTURE ROSES HEAD COACH

Drop the Struggle is a fabulous well-written, easy-to-understand book that can help you bring out the best version of you in life and sport. Alison and Jenna are skilled sport psychologists who tackle key mental skills in understanding yourself, your performance and life; they are underpinned by the Acceptance and Commitment Therapy (ACT) theory. A fascinating read with lots of techniques for personal growth. I couldn't put it down and can't wait to try some of the techniques myself!

PAUL THOMPSON MBE, COACH OF WORLD AND OLYMPIC ROWING CHAMPIONS

Psychology doesn't have to feel like something remote and academic; nor should it involve forcing yourself to think in a particular way. *Drop the Struggle* is a great place to understand how instead to work alongside your way of thinking, and maximise you at your best.

ANNIE VERNON OLY, OLYMPIC SILVER MEDALLIST AND WORLD CHAMPION ROWER, AWARD-WINNING AUTHOR OF MIND GAMES

Acceptance and commitment therapy applied to sports psychology is genius! *Drop the Struggle* should be in the kit bag of every student-athlete and on the bedside table of every coach and every athlete-parent.

DR PIPPA GRANGE, PSYCHOLOGIST AND CULTURE COACH

Understanding how your mind works and how to unlock your true potential – in sport and in life – is a transformational journey to embark on. In this incredibly powerful and practical book, Jenna and Alison will help you find your path as you learn the skills to stop struggling and start thriving. A game changer!

KATIE MOBED, OLYMPIC SPORT PSYCHOLOGIST

A fantastic book and an ideal training companion that can easily fit into your kit bag. Drop the Struggle *provides a toolkit that enables you to challenge thoughts and feelings and use them positively to obtain the skills required to achieve your goals, transforming the impossible into the possible.*

NICKI KELLY, WORLD RECORD HOLDER AND OCEAN ROWER

This is the book that I wish I'd been given when I was younger. An accessible guide and tool that makes the psychological side of the game that little bit less daunting. Having had the pleasure of working with both Alison and Jenna before, I look forward to applying their expertise to my work, life and sport once more.

ADAM WILSON, CHAIR OF BEHIND EVERY KICK

This is an amazing resource for all sportspeople, from the Olympian to a junior athlete. It gives the reader a completely different way to think about the mental side of sport. I am really looking forward to applying it to people I work with.

GREG SEARLE, OLYMPIC GOLD MEDALLIST AND INSPIRATIONAL SPEAKER

Love this book and wish I had it years ago to give to those starting their sporting career! A hugely practical, positive and progressive guide for anyone navigating the ups and downs of their sporting journey. Athletes and non-athletes alike will be inspired to change their mindset on performance – through the thoughtful explanations, impactful practices and encouraging case studies. This book clearly signposts the way to becoming a better performer.

NEASA RUSSELL, PARALYMPICS IRELAND SPORTS DIRECTOR AND CHEF DE MISSION (PARIS 2024)

Drop the Struggle gives you a great set of tools to help on your journey. Very clear and relatable, it is sure to be of use to anybody looking to improve the mental side of their life.

BEN TAYLOR-MATTHEWS, HEAD PROFESSIONAL, BRISTOL REAL TENNIS CLUB

Implementing the acceptance and commitment approach outlined in Drop the Struggle in my own leadership career has had an immeasurable impact. The Yellow Tail Moth story is particularly poignant, learning to accept my feelings and my own vulnerability as a leader. I progressed quickly into my current Chief of Staff role with an ease and confidence I had never felt before. And now I have a huge toolkit of strategies for when I get knocked off course, as I no doubt will in the future.

GILLIAN ORMSTON, CHIEF OF STAFF, THAMES VALLEY OFFICE FOR THE POLICE AND CRIME COMMISSIONER

A practical guide in simple language that makes sports psychology accessible and understandable for all. A worthy addition to any kit bag whether you are an athlete, coach, parent or anyone else who wants to reach their potential.

JOELIE CHISHOLM, COO GB SNOWSPORT

Jenna and Alison have used the tools from Drop the Struggle with coaches and players across the pathway at Saracens Mavericks. We've seen the positive impact on wellbeing and performance that this approach has. Recommended reading for all netballers!

SACHEL GRANT, PERFORMANCE PATHWAY LEAD, SARACENS MAVERICKS

DROP *the* STRUGGLE

DROP *the* STRUGGLE

A transformative approach to achieving your potential in sport and life

DR ALISON MAITLAND AND JENNA ASHFORD

SEQUOIA BOOKS

First published in 2023 by Sequoia Books

ISBN
Print: 9781914110269
EPUB: 9781914110276

A CIP record for this book is available from the British Library

Library of Congress Cataloguing-In-Publication Data

Name: Alison Maitland & Jenna Ashford
Title: Drop the Struggle/Maitland & Ashford
Description: 1st Edition, Sequoia Books UK 2023
Subjects: B: Philosophy, Psychology, Religion
Print: 9781914110269
EPUB: 9781914110276

Library of Congress Control Number: 2023916300

Print and Electronic production managed by Deanta Global

For Helen Cunningham who believed that the only boundaries are the ones we put there ourselves.
And for Ivy Ashford, who has her whole life ahead of her. Let this book remind you to make those boundaries limitless.

Contents

Introduction   1

Out with the old, in with the new 2
Taking action (this bit is really important!) 3
Who we are 4
Time to reflect 8

Part I   Developing your skills

1   Your Thinking and Observing Mind   11

Our brain is built for survival 11
Thinking vs Observing Mind 14
Get to know your two minds 16
What's in your kitbag? 20

2   Play in the now   22

Time-travelling thoughts 23
How well do you stay in the moment? 24
Getting practical about being mindful 25
Grounding and stabilising our thoughts 28
Playing in the now requires practice 28
Flexing your attention 31
Think of it like training Matty 34
What's in your kitbag? 35

3   Drop the struggle with your thoughts   37

What are thoughts? 38
Dropping the struggle 40
Getting better at dropping the struggle 43
What's in your kitbag? 50

4   Accept being uncomfortable   51

   We all face pressure 51
   The relationship between pressure and performance 53
   Our response to pressure is the problem 56
   Are you willing to do something different? 58
   The struggle switch 60
   Saying yes to your feelings 61
   What's in your kitbag? 66

5   Do what matters   68

   The journey ahead 68
   The destination – where am I going? 69
   The purpose – why am I going on a journey? 71
   Finding your Values Compass 75
   How do I get there? My sport roadmap 78
   Make a commitment 82
   What is holding you back? 83
   What's in your kitbag? 84

Part II   Applying the training

6   The confidence choice   89

   The truth about confidence 89
   Do what matters: Confidence as an action 92
   Drop the struggle: It's normal to doubt yourself 94
   Play in the now: Pay attention 97
   Accept being uncomfortable: The stuck loop 99
   What's in your kitbag? 101

7   Create the energy to succeed   103

   Using the Values Compass for motivation 104
   Do what matters: Focus on small actions 108
   Drop the struggle: Give your mind a name 114
   Accept being uncomfortable: Urge Surfing 116
   Play in the now: Move in slow motion 119
   What's in your kitbag? 120

8   Embrace setbacks and failure   122

Setbacks are to learn from 122
Drop the struggle: I am not my story 124
Accept being uncomfortable: The discomfort of setbacks 127
Play in the now: Drop anchor 129
Do what matters: Go in the right direction 131
What's in your kitbag? 134

9   The onward journey   136

Enjoy the journey 136
Choose to stay on track with The Choice Point 138
A dose of self-compassion when things don't go to plan 145
Pack your kitbag 147
Time to dream big 149

Notes   153
Index   159

Introduction

Whatever it is that has brought you to this book, welcome.

You are here because you're involved in sport. You want to overcome some of the mental challenges that inevitably come with the highs and lows of sporting performance.

You might have a particular challenge that you are grappling with – lack of confidence, fear of failure, inconsistency, a mental block or simply feeling you're not fulfilling your potential. Or perhaps you are a coach, partner, parent or supporter of an athlete who is struggling with mental barriers.

It's a frustrating place to be. We are here to help.

If you've tried to get over your mental hurdle, you might be confused and frustrated about why your efforts are not leading to any consistent changes. Or it may be that you have been burying your head in the sand for a while, hoping that one day you'll wake up and be miraculously free from the psychological struggle.

Either way, the important thing is that you've picked up this book. You've done the hard part. Now is the time for change.

This is a book for anyone, no matter your level or your sport, no matter your previous experiences with psychology and no matter what your starting point is.

We are here to help you find a long-term solution to your current challenges. To *Drop the Struggle* while keeping hold of all the things necessary to perform at your best. This book will teach you a sustainable way of dealing with difficult thoughts, managing your emotions and harnessing them to help you perform to the best of your ability, as often as possible.

The solutions in this book are not quick, short-term fixes. You'll have to do something different. You must let go of old ways of thinking and step into new thought patterns. Think of it like a journey up a mountain, you are at the bottom, looking up. It seems daunting, and you're not sure if it's even possible. This book encourages you to take the first few steps and see what a difference it makes. If you find that the journey is rewarding, you may choose to continue. You will likely veer off the path, trip up and want to turn back. But that's all part of the journey. And with persistence and an open mind, you will make it to the top. It will be worth it.

Out with the old, in with the new

Much of traditional sport psychology focusses on positive thinking. Great if you are able to think positively in your current situation, but what if you're not? What if you've been injured and have to take time out, or you've been dropped or excluded from a squad? Or perhaps you are making mistake after mistake, but know you are better than that. You may be suffering from crippling nerves or a loss of confidence, and all the thoughts you have are negative ones.

No matter how much we tell you positive thinking helps, the wonderful machine that is your mind will take your thoughts in all different directions. We are not going to go over old techniques like visualisation, boosting your self-esteem, challenging negative thoughts or relaxation. While these have their place, we want you to try something new. Through research[1] and our own experiences, we now know that there is another way; another way that can and will transform your life and sporting career if you work hard to make it happen.

The technical term for the approach you will learn in this book is Acceptance and Commitment Therapy (ACT).

We will explore what this means; but for now, just know that ACT interventions have shown to lead to higher levels of performance[2] and improved general psychological well-being.[3]

This book isn't about getting rid of thoughts or feelings, but it's about changing your relationship with them. *Drop the Struggle* isn't about removing thoughts from our mind or feelings from our body; it's about handling them more effectively, so they don't stop us from being the athlete we want to be. That way we can train and compete to the very best of our ability. From our experience, it's hard to enjoy what you are doing while you're trying *not* to think about something. You can't be your best self if you are attempting to escape from certain thoughts or feelings.

Let's do a quick experiment. You'll need a pen for this ...

1. Complete the sentence: 'the thoughts and feelings I'd most like to get rid of are ...'
2. Now write a list of a few things you've tried in order to avoid or get rid of these.
3. Go through each item and ask yourself: 'did it get rid of the thought or feeling?' and 'did it help me to perform better in the long term?'

If the answer is 'no' to either or both of the last two questions, that's a real sign that doing something different is in order.

Taking action (this bit is really important!)

Imagine that we walked with you into a gym and showed you around the state-of-the-art equipment. We talked through how to use the machines and even stood and watched some of the fittest people at the gym in action. Would you expect to get fitter by doing that? No, of course, you wouldn't.

It's the same with your mind. Progress takes practice. Practice starts with being open-minded to the learning process and leads to throwing yourself in, having a go and trying what you learn in this book out there in the 'real world'. It involves reflecting and learning from what works and what doesn't and adjusting what you do next as a result. It involves sticking it out, even when it's hard, and pushes you outside of your comfort zone, or even when you think it's not 'working'.

You'll come across various exercises to complete throughout this book. Some of them just require you to pause and think, others require you to make a note of your thoughts and actions. Along with some key ideas, these will form the basis of your psychology 'kitbag' going forward.

Take some time to consider what mindset and behaviours you need to bring to reading this book and transforming yourself. It may be that you commit to reading one chapter a week, or that you practise a new strategy every month.

Getting the most out of this book ...

- Pause, give yourself time and headspace to understand and develop your mind
- Look inward, asking yourself questions and taking time to answer them
- Complete the exercises throughout this book with thought and care
- Practise the skills and tools you like the best
- Share your learnings with others, and discuss what you're finding out about yourself
- Have a notebook to record your thoughts and reflections

Who we are

It feels important to let you know who we are, who is behind this book.

Jenna Ashford

My sport was hockey. I played right from when I was young, following in my dad and brother's footsteps. I captained my school team and the county squad; at the age of 15, I got my first cap for England. I continued to represent England in various international tournaments until the age of 21. I then went to play in the German Bundesliga and Australian 1st League. I played in the English Premier League for 13 years and won the league title seven times. Hockey enabled me to travel, focussed my mind and gave me such amazing friendships. On the face of it, it sounds like a great sporting career.

Underneath it, however, there is a story that 'I never quite made it'. I was labelled 'the talented one' from a very young age and was the best in most of the teams that I played in. I enjoyed it, loved being outside and playing with my friends; I was naturally good at it and things seemed to be going in the right direction. But somewhere down the line, I lost the love for the sport, my motivation dipped, and I found myself going through the motions without really knowing why I was doing it or what I wanted to achieve. This reflected in my hockey, as my peers started to overtake me and then sail past. I realised that the 'talent' I once had was not enough to get me to the top, and I no longer had the desire to put in the work and dedication that was needed. I watched as some of my former teammates and friends made it to the Olympics, winning the ultimate prize of a Gold Medal in the 2016 Rio Games, as I stepped away from the sport.

Yet that's not the end of the story. My sporting experiences, the highs and the lows, sparked my fascination with the mind and how powerful it could be. I wanted to know more about the key ingredients needed to be a happy and successful sportsperson. This interest ultimately led me to seek out a career as a sport psychologist, working with young people just setting out on their sports journey, to those at the height of their sporting endeavours, right through to those retiring from a career in sport. This includes working with England Football teams, GB rowers, national tennis players, the British Army, corporate organisations, CEOs of global companies as well as many schools across the country.

Sport taught me so much – about myself, about life, about other people. But it can also be a cruel place, filled with uncertainty, rejection and loss. As I look back on my hockey career now, I can be proud of what I achieved. And most of all, I am proud of where it has led me to – having a career helping others to get the best out of themselves – both in and away from the sports arena. I am driven by helping others understand their minds better, so that they can enjoy the highs and work through the lows – recognising them as an inevitable but crucial part of both sport and life.

Dr Alison Maitland

Although my great-grandfather captained the England men's football team, winning 41 caps, my family had no sporting expectations for me. I loved trying my hand at all sports, playing county-level netball and lacrosse, but eventually landed on athletics as a teenager. I dreamed of going to the Olympics one day.

My plans started well as I competed in national competitions almost straight away. Yet I never quite believed in myself, feeling wracked with nerves before even the most mundane of events, as I struggled to control my thoughts and feelings. My favourite mantra was 'I could have run faster'.

I finished competing in my late 20s, spending many years after that wondering how I could have better enjoyed my running career and reached my potential. And it was that curiosity that led me to retrain as a sport psychologist, working with others to explore – how do you deal with competitive anxiety, what stops people from backing themselves, how do you focus on what you want to achieve?

I've worked with club and Olympic rowers, with junior, pathway and Superleague netball teams and in the fascinating world of real tennis, walking alongside coaches, athletes and parents. It's only now I understand that the focus on controlling our thoughts and feelings is upside down. Teaming up with Jenna to apply an Acceptance and Commitment approach is like finding the secret in the secret sauce – we can't control our minds or our feelings! It's what we do, not what we think or feel, that makes the difference between never being satisfied with our sport journey, or stepping out and getting the most from it. When you learn this, the world of sport opens up.

Ultimately, we are athletes and coaches just like you. We started out playing sport just for fun, realised we were quite good at it and dedicated much of our lives to it. We have been through the highs of winning and the despair of failure.

We may not have been in your exact boat, but we have sailed in one pretty similar!

Now, we are sport psychologists, working with athletes and high-performance individuals from all fields of life. Helping them to overcome the challenges that living a life of chasing excellence can bring. But most of all, we are ordinary people who have stumbled across a method that we want to share with as many athletes and coaches as we can. We know it works, we have benefited from it first hand in our own lives and have also seen how it has helped many others to overcome mental barriers and reach a level of performance and contentment they didn't know was possible.

Think of us like your mountain guides. You're about to start climbing a big mountain, and our job is to watch out for you and shout out directions when we see places you might slip, miss a path or go down a dead end. We don't know exactly what it feels like to climb your mountain (only you know that), but we can help you to see where you are about to step, and the different routes you might take as you ascend.

Time to reflect

When light from an object is reflected by a surface, it changes direction. When we reflect on our own experiences, it allows us to change direction too.

We want to end this chapter, not by telling you anything else, but by asking you some questions. We encourage you to take some time to pause and reflect.

What do you want to achieve in your sport?

Why do you want to invest time in reading this book and developing yourself?

If this book transformed you, what would you be doing differently in one-year's time?

PART I

Developing your skills

Imagine you are behind a closed door. On the other side are all your hopes, dreams and aspirations.

Right here, on this side of the closed door, are the things you struggle with. All the unhelpful thoughts and feelings that you often get caught up in (the inner critic, the I'm not good enough, fast enough, tall enough, strong enough stories, along with the accompanying feelings such as anxiety, fear or embarrassment). You don't like being on this side of the door. It's uncomfortable. You spend most of the time wanting to run away from these thoughts and feelings and maybe quit your sport or at least not try so hard. Or you spend all your energy trying to fight these thoughts and feelings, worrying about what has happened in the past or might happen in the future, instead of enjoying what you are doing right now. But if you stay here, caught up in the unhelpful thoughts and feelings and don't learn how to open the door and walk through to the other side, you'll find it hard to fulfil your potential.

To open the door and walk through you need to be willing to investigate what you are capable of, explore what is unknown, and be open to what's possible. We have to step into the challenges of being an athlete and situations that take us out of our comfort zone.

This means learning something new.

You'll learn how to unhook from these unhelpful thoughts and feelings (*Drop the Struggle*), how to make space for them however uncomfortable they may be (*Accept Being Uncomfortable*), how to be mindful and stay in the present (*Play in the Now*) and how to change your behaviour, set a direction and take steps towards your dreams (*Do What Matters*).

These skills will be crucial to helping the door swing open more easily – think of them like items in your kitbag. As you get better at using them, a whole raft of possibilities will open up to you in sport. You'll be able to delve in your kitbag for tools to help you respond more effectively when the training is tough or decisions don't go the way you planned. You'll grow and develop as an athlete and more often be able to behave like the sportsperson you want to be.

Before you learn these skills, in Chapter 1 let's begin by getting to know how your mind works, so you can start to notice the thoughts and feelings you struggle with and that hold you back.

Chapter 1

Your Thinking and Observing Mind

You can observe a lot just by watching.
YOGI BERRA[1]

To make a long-term shift in our performance, first, we need to know our mind better, to understand both how and why we think.

Our brain is built for survival

Have you ever wondered why, even when things are going really well in your life or in your sport, your mind still finds ways to be negative?

Or just when you think you have your nerves under control, you suddenly feel panicked and can't remember what you're supposed to be doing?

Or you do so much positive thinking and visualisation that you feel like the most positive person in the world, yet it all goes out the window when it comes to the pressure of competition?

Or you can't stop comparing yourself to other people in the squad and it puts you off really committing to training?

Well, it's because that's how we have evolved. Luckily *and* unluckily for us, our minds are experts at scanning for threats and events that might harm us. Back when we were cavewomen and cavemen and life was very dangerous, this part of our brain was incredibly important. Our own survival was based on our ability to spot things that might harm us. If we weren't good at predicting or spotting danger, it didn't end well. So, it's lucky for us that our mind continually searched for things that might hurt us, because it often saved our life.

Similarly, cave people relied on being part of a tribe or community to survive. We had to quickly learn to fit in with the group behaviours and norms, or we would be ostracised and left to fend for ourselves. Back then, being outside the group put us in real danger.

The modern world is of course very different. Although we generally have far fewer threats to our lives in our immediate surroundings, our minds are still operating as if we could be under attack at any minute. Being part of a tribe is not so necessary for hunting food, but our minds still spend long hours comparing ourselves to other people, worrying that we are not contributing or fitting in. Our mind shuttles back and forth, time-travelling between the past and the future, causing us to worry, predict the worst and overthink even small things.

Helpful for survival. Not so helpful for peak performance or a happy, peaceful and fulfilled life.

This explains why it's often hard to feel 100% satisfied in sport, even after a victory. Our cave-person mind had the belief that no matter how much you already had, you needed more to have a better chance of survival. Got 1 kg of berries? Well, 2 kg is better – keep going! Sharpened your tools to keep yourself safe? There might be an even bigger predator we don't know about, so keep sharpening.

Translate that to today, and you've won an event you've been training months for. You thought it would bring about a level of satisfaction you've never had before. And maybe it did for a short time, but that fades away and you're left thinking 'what's next?' The brief moment of internal pride and satisfaction is quickly surpassed by 'I need to be better or else it won't last'. There remains an intense desire to improve, be better than others and be better than we were yesterday. In itself, this isn't necessarily a bad thing. Indeed, to be successful in sport you need to work immensely hard, push boundaries and challenge yourself to your limits. On a good day, this feels like motivation, focus and drive. You can feel the progress you're making and relish the sense of mastery that you experience as a result. But on a bad day, you can easily fall into the trap of wanting more recognition, better scores and faster times, no matter what you achieve. This can feel like dissatisfaction, discontent and inadequacy. It can seem like nothing you ever do is good enough, and that everyone around you is overtaking you. It is exhausting never to be satisfied with where you have got to and demoralising to think that you may never 'get there'.

And this is your mind in all its glory, doing what it was built to do ... be on high alert for how it can keep you safe from danger, in the crowd and wanting more.

Your reason-giving generator

To keep you safe, your mind is also a brilliant reason-giving generator. As soon as you want to do something that's important to you, it cranks out a load of reasons why you can't or shouldn't do it.

Which of these statements do you recognise from your own mind?

- Obstacles
  'It's raining'
  'I haven't got time today'
- Self-judgements
  'I'm lazy'
  'I give up too easily'
- Comparisons
  'I'll never be as good as them'

'They are so much more confident than I am'
- Predictions
  'There's no point, I won't get picked anyway'
  'I'll probably come last'

What else does your mind say under these headings? Write down a few more. Recognising it is the first step to doing something about it!

Unfortunately, these thought patterns are inevitable. Our mind often finds obstacles to why we can't perform, judges ourselves negatively, holds us back with comparisons to other athletes or predicts that our performance is doomed to fail. It is just how minds work.

The big question is, how do we deal with it?

Well in order to answer this question, first we want to introduce you to two different parts of your mind that you will get to know very well by the end of this book.

Thinking vs Observing Mind

As you sit there now, give yourself 30 seconds to do nothing. Put the book down, set a timer and just let your mind go wherever it wants.

What happened? Your mind started wandering. 'Oh damn I forgot to put the washing out' … 'what will I have for dinner' … 'can't believe she said that' …

Welcome to your Thinking Mind!

Your Thinking Mind is all your thoughts, judgements, opinions, reasons, memories and beliefs. It wanders around and goes wherever it wants to go.

Our Thinking Mind can be really helpful. For example, it helps us to solve complex problems such as 'what move should I make next?' or 'where can I place the next pass?' It's also brilliant at helping us to communicate with our teammates and look into the future so we can plan our training to reach our goals.

What you also need to know about your Thinking Mind is that you can't control it. You can't stop the thoughts that come and go, however much you try. In fact, often, the harder you try NOT to think about something, the more you think about it. That's the downside of our Thinking Mind.

Your worst sporting memory

Pause here for a moment to think about your worst ever sporting memory. Imagine yourself back there, what happened and how you felt. Who was there? What made it so bad?

Now erase that memory from your mind. Try and completely forget about it, as if it didn't exist.

Pretty hard right? No matter how hard you try to forget it, it will still be there.

So we are sports psychologists telling you that you can't control your thoughts. Really?

Yes, really.

If you can't control them, how can you stop all this unhelpful mind chatter that gets in the way of you performing at your best or being the person you want to be?

This is where another part of your mind comes in – it's called your Observing Mind. When you catch yourself thinking negatively or worrying about something unnecessarily, the part of you that catches yourself is your Observing Mind. It's the part of you that can step back and watch your thoughts. The part of you that notices you feel pain in your body or observes a sensation. It doesn't judge, or criticise or blame. It just notices.

Your Observing Mind is like a camera filming a wildlife documentary. When the lion chases the antelope, the camera doesn't judge it as good or bad, it simply records what happens.

Notice who's noticing

Just for a moment turn your attention to your breath. Notice the air coming in and going out through your nose. Do this for several breaths. Carry on noticing your breath. Notice how the air is slightly cooler when you breathe it in, and slightly warmer when you breathe it out ... there is your breath and there you are, noticing your breath.

Get to know your two minds

Let's bring this back into the sports domain. Imagine a tennis player who is in the middle of a match, and truly focussed. Now, suppose thoughts start popping into their head like, 'I hope my grip is correct', 'I'd better make this a good shot' or 'Wow, that ball is moving fast!' That is their Thinking Mind at work. The Observing Mind is what notices all these thoughts.

Most of the time, we get sucked into our Thinking Mind and get caught up in everything that goes in and out of it. We pay attention to it and wholeheartedly believe everything it says. If your Thinking Mind tells you 'I am not good enough to be here', you believe it. Or 'today just isn't my day', you buy into it.

Most of our worry, stress and underperformance comes from the fact that we are totally absorbed in our Thinking Mind and not making use of our Observing Mind.

When people ask us 'how do I stop feeling nervous' or 'how do I stop thinking about failure', our answer is: you don't. You can't control that wonderful Thinking Mind of yours and get it to stop thinking or feeling. As soon as you try to not think or feel something, not only does the thought or feeling not go away, you also tend to make it even stronger.

What you can do is utilise your Observing Mind to your advantage, to become more aware of your thoughts and to *Drop the Struggle* with them.

The inflatable beach ball

Imagine that you are in a swimming pool. You have a big inflatable beach ball and you're trying to push it under the surface of the water.

What does that feel like?

Hard work isn't it! And then as soon as you let go, what happens? It pops right back up in your face!

Your unwanted thoughts are like this too. Trying to push them away, get rid of them or pretend they are not there is exhausting. And it doesn't really work, because eventually they will pop back up even louder and stronger than before.

So what we are suggesting is, instead of pushing the beach ball under the water, just let it float around the pool. It can be there, but you don't have to engage with it. Your unwanted thoughts can be there, but you don't need to believe them or act on them.

What we are teaching you is *not* to think differently, we are teaching you skills to handle difficult thoughts and feelings more effectively, so they have less of an impact on you and the things you want to do as an athlete.

From here on, you won't hear us refer to thoughts as negative. We will call them unhelpful, critical or judgemental. Because, how can we know if a thought is positive or negative?

'If I make this decision, it's most likely to go wrong'. That's a thought we might judge to be negative, but it could actually be pretty helpful!

Or the thought 'I'm the best, no one can beat me' is perhaps one we'd class as positive, but might actually lead to complacency and have negative effects on performance.

So we prefer to think about thoughts and feelings as being helpful or unhelpful, rather than positive or negative. A thought itself isn't negative or positive; it's whether we react to it automatically in rigid, unhelpful ways that make the situation worse and take us away from being the athlete we want to be.

Tapping into your Observing Mind and learning to notice your thoughts helps you to realise that you don't have to be defined by those thoughts. They are just random images that pop in and out of your head, and you can choose whether you believe them or not. It creates a kind of separation from your thoughts so they don't pull you around and stop you doing the things you want to do.

When you go to the supermarket, do you buy everything or only pick what you want?

Of course, you just select the things you want that day. All the other items are still there – they don't disappear, they just stay on the shelf.

The same applies to life. Your thoughts are around all the time. You only need to pick the thoughts that are helpful to you. You don't need to listen to them all.

Separating your Observing Mind from your Thinking Mind is a skill that takes practice. But once you begin to do it, you'll feel yourself becoming less and less of a slave to your thoughts. Your ability to enjoy and thrive in your sport will reach a new level.

Here are some ideas to help you better identify your Observing Mind:

- Listen to the sounds around you. Simply notice what you hear.
- Watch your breath. Observe the sensation of inhaling and exhaling, noticing your belly rising and falling as you breathe.
- Notice any smells in your surroundings. Notice if you make any judgements about them, whether they are good or bad.
- Observe the feeling of the floor under your feet or the wind blowing on your face. Notice the sensations in your body and the thoughts that arise.
- Notice the way you are holding your body, maybe your facial expression or posture. Notice what it feels like, or which muscles are engaged.

A helpful way to think about our Observing and Thinking Mind is like the sky and the weather.

The sky and the weather[2]

Think of your Observing Mind as being like the sky, and your Thinking Mind as like the weather. The weather is constantly changing … sun one minute, rain the next and a thunderstorm rolling in behind. Despite this, the sky remains unchanged and unaffected. No matter how bad the weather gets, the sky always has room for it. What's more, the weather does not last forever, and the storm always passes in the end.

The sky is like the Observing Mind that is always there, making room for difficult thoughts and feelings coming from your Thinking Mind.

If you are able to, right now look up at the sky and take note of everything you can see.

The chances are that you are noticing clouds, birds, aeroplanes, the sun, stars or rain. It's very common for us all to notice the contents of the sky (what's passing through it at a given moment) but to lose sight of the actual sky itself – the space that contains these various elements. Did you find that you did that too?

When we experience strong emotions or unwanted thoughts, we often forget our Observing Mind, and instead see only our thoughts, feelings and sensations. We get caught up in the contents of our Thinking Mind. But just like the sky, our Observing Mind is always there, always present and seems to have room for any of the emotions or thoughts that pass through it.

What's in your kitbag?

Let's see what's in your kitbag so far.

First, we've discussed the mind. Not the anatomical parts of it, or the neuroscientific definition of what's in your brain, but a revolutionary, simple explanation of how and why we think. Knowing this forms the foundation of the book and will help you to understand and practise all the strategies we take you through.

You've also realised that you can't control your thoughts, so you might as well stop trying to do this. Instead, you explored how to use your Observing Mind to notice your Thinking Mind, and all the thoughts, feelings, sensations and urges it throws up for you. Remember, you are *not* learning how to think differently, but to handle difficult thoughts and feelings more *effectively*, so they have less of a negative impact on you.

So next time you are stepping up to take a penalty, catastrophising about an upcoming match, or in the depths of despair after a setback, sit back and use your Observing Mind to notice your Thinking Mind in action. If it's helpful, think of the Observing Mind as being like the sky and your thoughts and feelings generated by your Thinking Mind are like the weather. Once you've differentiated your two minds, you stop trying to control the weather. Instead, you can begin to evaluate your thoughts and feelings from an objective place and decide which ones are helpful and which ones are harmful to your performance.

You'll use your Observing Mind in Chapter 2 to stay present and mindfully make effective choices about what you do as an athlete. We call this *Play in the Now.*

Chapter *2*

Play in the now

Wherever you are, be there totally.
ECKHART TOLLE

If I were to analyse your thoughts for 30 minutes whilst you were competing in your sport, what percentage of those thoughts would you say were:

(a) about the past (such as a mistake you made in the first few minutes)
(b) in the present (what's happening right here, right now)
(c) about the future (such as what will happen if you don't score, or your plans for the rest of the day)
(d) about ... I have no idea what I was thinking for the last 30 minutes.

Research suggests that we spend as much time thinking about the past and the future than we do about what's going on right now. One study that collected 250,000 data points on participants' thoughts, feelings and actions as they went about their lives found that people spend 46.9% of their waking hours thinking about something other than what they're doing.[1]

Then comes the question, how does this affect performance?

Let's consider Jamie, an 18-year-old rugby player we worked with. He rose up the ranks quickly and was soon playing his debut for the first team. Going into the match, he was crippled with nerves, imagining all the things he might get wrong in the game. He wanted to get through it as quickly as possible. It was all a blur and when he got to the end, he could hardly remember anything about it. He knew that he wasn't at his best and spent much of the game getting caught up in thoughts such as 'I shouldn't do this in case …' and 'I wonder what the team is thinking about my performance' which detracted from his ability to both enjoy the game and play well.

This is a scenario many of us will recognise. That's our Thinking Mind doing what it's good at – thinking, planning, problem-solving and analysing. In this chapter, we'll learn that the time-travelling thoughts of our Thinking Mind make it really hard to focus or *Play in the Now*. By practising the skill of mindfulness, we can really increase our ability to be present and bring our focus back each time it drifts. Staying focussed on the here and now helps us to make more effective choices and bring our best possible performance each and every time we train and compete.

Time-travelling thoughts

Whilst it's incredibly irritating, these time-travelling thoughts are merely our Thinking Mind trying to protect us. As we explored in Chapter 1, the ability to think about the past or the future is very helpful. Going over previous events means we can learn from them, and back in the days of our ancient ancestors, this may have saved our lives. Considering every possible negative future scenario is evolution's way of keeping us alive by planning for what might go wrong. It allows us to be more prepared, and to solve problems. However, because there is a lot less physical threat nowadays, this time-travelling Thinking Mind is overactive to the point of being unhelpful. It's all too easy to let our minds pull us around with very little awareness of what's happening. It's the ability to recognise that our Thinking Mind has gone elsewhere; gently bring it back to the here and now which is the key to greater levels of focus, performance and enjoyment in sport.

Imagine for a moment that you are trying to play badminton, and there is a big annoying fly following you around wherever you go. It's really close to your face and will not leave you alone, however much you try to swat it away. It's so loud and annoying you can't think straight, focus on your opponent or hear the umpire. This fly would make it difficult to perform at your best, wouldn't it? Focussing on what you were supposed to do would be a challenge, and the irritating fly would be a constant distraction, pulling your attention away from your performance.

It's a bit like this when we get caught up in our Thinking Mind and become hooked by our thoughts and feelings. It's impossible to focus or be in the present moment as our attention is taken away from all the things it would be helpful to focus on. As a result, our performance suffers.

The ability to *Play in the Now* – to be mindful – doesn't make the fly go away, it just helps it to fly further away in the distance. It means you can focus on the thoughts and actions that matter, whilst allowing other, less helpful thoughts, to float in the background. It's the ability to place importance on the thoughts and actions you want to, rather than letting your Thinking Mind decide for itself.

How well do you stay in the moment?

In Chapter 1, we asked you how skillful you were at keeping your mind in the present. Maybe that was a fluke? Have a go at this exercise to see how well you do now.

One minute focus

Bring to mind your favourite book, film or TV programme. Think about some details, such as the name, location, characters and storyline.

Then for one minute, think only about the book, film or TV programme you have chosen. Don't think about anything else. 100% focus on it. One minute – go!

How well did you do? Did you manage to think about that single thing for the whole 60 seconds? Chances are your mind wandered off several times.

It's hard to stay present – even when we have nothing else to distract us. Our Thinking Mind takes us all over the place. It's trying to make sense of things; it's ruminating and worrying; it's being critical; it's giving us rules to act on; it's judgemental; it gets stuck on an endless groundhog day loop replaying the same thoughts and feelings over and over again.

Thankfully, the skill of being and staying present can be developed. This is mindfulness.

Getting practical about being mindful

The sceptics among you may associate mindfulness with sitting cross-legged on the floor, or going into a dark room to meditate by yourself for hours on end; or you may think that mindfulness is about simply relaxing until you fall asleep.

In reality, being mindful is a lot more than this, and it's something that can be incorporated into everything you do, in and away from sport.

What mindfulness is	What mindfulness isn't
• Mindfulness simply entails paying attention to what is going on, including the things that are challenging for us. • It is using your Observing Mind to pay attention to your thoughts, physical sensations and environment, without judgement on what's happening, or trying to make it other than what it is. • It is a way of bringing your wandering thoughts and Thinking Mind back to the present moment.	• It isn't a meditation practice. Meditation is part of being mindful, but mindfulness is a practice for the whole of life. • It isn't about emptying your mind. As we've learnt, minds produce thoughts – it's what they're built for. Mindfulness is about becoming aware of these thoughts and learning to let them go. • It's not about always feeling good. In reality, it's about recognising and acknowledging your feelings, anxieties, pains and challenges, and working with them without judgement.

If we were to put mindfulness into a simple formula,[2] it would look like this:

Mindfulness = Notice X

Noticing is paying attention to, focussing on or bringing your awareness to X, where X is:

- anything that's present in this moment, for example, a thought, feeling, sensation, urge, memory … OR …

- anything you can see, hear, touch, taste or smell, for example, the sight of your racket or oar, the sensation of wind on your face, the action of kicking a ball, the taste of a salty sweat, the splash of the rain on your hands.

You can be mindful doing just about any activity. All you have to do is bring your attention to the here and now, notice when your mind wanders and bring it back again to the present.

Let's use an activity we do all the time when we train and compete – taking a sip of liquid to rehydrate ourselves – to practise being in the here and now. Try this exercise.

A mindful sip[3]

Make sure you have some water in your bottle. Then sit and get comfortable.

Bring your attention inside and give yourself permission to take one minute for yourself. Take three deep breaths and exhale slowly for each breath to empty your lungs, and on the last breath put your hand on your bottle.

After your third breath, shift your gaze to the water. Notice the weight of the bottle in your hand. Notice the water and how calm it is. Gently move the bottle and notice the water swirl around.

If your mind is jumping around, it's okay. Be patient; this is normal. The aim here is to transition your mind from the busy world to the now.

Take the water to your mouth slowly and take a sip as slowly as you can. Let the water stay inside your mouth without swallowing. Feel the water against your cheeks. Pay attention to the space it fills in your mouth. And then as slow as you can, swallow it. Notice the sound of you swallowing.

Whenever you notice your attention has wandered, acknowledge it, then refocus on the exercise.

Run through this a couple more times with the intention of focussing as much of your attention as possible on the water and the drinking.

We can guarantee your Thinking Mind will have done a lot of wandering as you did this practice. You will have had to bring it back to focus on the water several times.

Grounding and stabilising our thoughts

To help you develop this skill, it can be useful to have an anchor. An anchor is a place that you can return to when your mind wanders off, to bring you back to the present moment. A clear anchor can secure your focus and restore your attention when you are distracted by thoughts.

An anchor helps being present become practical. It's not focussing on nothing; it's focussing on something. It's clear and tangible and is something that you can continually work on – you will never be perfectly mindful.

The breath is one of the strongest anchors, because it's with you always (we will come onto this shortly). In the mindful sip exercise, you used the liquid in your bottle as an anchor, always bringing your attention back to that liquid if your mind drifted off. Other anchors include bodily sensations, or anything you can hear, smell, taste, touch or see.

When you get wrapped up in your thoughts and your Observing Mind is aware that your Thinking Mind is busy, you need simply focus your attention on your anchor to bring you back to the present moment.

Athletes we have worked with have used a variety of anchors during sporting performance; wiping their face with a towel (tennis), stepping over a line (rugby), three deep breaths before entering the pool (swimming) and tightening and releasing their grip (hockey). What's important is to find one that works for you and reminds you to bring your attention back to the here and now.

Playing in the now requires practice

Getting better at being mindful whilst you play and compete requires practice.

One of the easiest and most effective ways to be mindful is using your breath. Your breath is something you have with you all of the time and is also the only bodily function that you can do both consciously and unconsciously. Whilst we spend much of our life on autopilot, distracted by all our thoughts and missing what's really going on, the breath is always there. Yet most of the time, we aren't even aware of it.

Mindful breathing can be an enormously powerful skill for your mental and physical well-being as well as sporting performance.[4] More widely, research has shown that using the breath in mindfulness and meditation can increase happiness, strengthen the immune system, relieve anxiety and increase focus, among many other benefits.[5]

The famous Wim Hof, holder of over 25 Guinness world records, uses meditative breathing techniques to do incredible things, like climbing Mount Everest wearing only shorts, freezing himself in ice for hours on end and running barefoot marathons in the Arctic Circle.[6]

There are many techniques that will teach you to breathe in a certain way, using your diaphragm, or at a certain pace. Mindful breathing isn't about controlling your breathing, or breathing in a certain way or in a particular part of the body. It is simply noticing. That's all you have to do – notice your breath.

Try this exercise to develop mindful breathing. For a recording of the exercise, head to https://www.yellowtailgroup.co.uk/team-4. Or if you have a willing friend, ask them to read it to you.

Mindful breathing

As you stand (or sit) with your feet on the floor, notice the sensation of your feet in your shoes. Now bring your attention to your breath, noticing the rise and fall of your chest. Now notice the sensations of your feet on the floor.

Notice any tension in your legs, arms, hands, shoulders and face, gently letting it go. Bring the attention back to the breath for the moment.

Now expand your awareness to any sounds around you. Perhaps you may not have been aware of small sounds like a hum, people talking or nature. Simply notice these sounds.

Keep your attention on the sounds whilst also noticing the breath

Focus back on your breathing. Breathe in through your nose and out through your nose. Bring your attention to the air coming in and going out of your nostrils. Notice how the air coming out is ever so slightly warmer than the air coming in. Notice the distribution of air between both nostrils – is it even?

Continue in this way for as long as you want without guidance. Simply watch and notice your breath.

If a thought pops up, just notice it and acknowledge it and refocus your attention back on your breath.

No matter how much we practise staying in the moment, we all have times when our mind wanders, and we are caught up in our thoughts. However, there are many opportunities when we are competing or training when we can break state, reset our minds, focus and come back into the present. It could be at half-time, before being subbed onto the pitch, at a short corner, when the ball goes out of play, paddling up to start a race or at a lap marker for example.

Everyday mindfulness

Take some time to explore what other activities could be done mindfully in your life and your sport. Maybe it's tying your shoelaces, putting your kit on, passing the ball from one hand to another, stepping onto the pitch or court, going through your last bits of preparation, taking a deep breath before you start. The list of actions you can do mindfully is endless. Choose your own favourites.

Flexing your attention

Clinical psychologist Steven Hayes recounts the story of a small boat sailor he met on a plane journey. This sailor had fantastic success as a racer, particularly in his hometown of New Orleans. Assuming this success must have been down to his knowledge of the local currents or the prevailing winds, Hayes was surprised when his new-found acquaintance leaned in and whispered to him, 'All the locals know the winds and the currents … I smell the coffee'. New Orleans is the second largest coffee port in the United States. Along the coast are a few coffee-roasting plants. Each plant roasts a particular bean with its own special qualities and its own very distinctive aroma. As he was racing, all the sailor had to do was to notice the unique smell of a specific coffee bean to know the wind direction. His well-trained nose and experience of the coastline enabled him to be aware of the tiniest change in the wind just by being mindful of the smell of coffee and hence gain a competitive advantage. As Hayes says, who would think they could smell their way to winning a sailing race?

In this story, the sailor's ability to be in the present as he competed enormously increased the amount of information available to him. He was able to focus on sailing his boat, *and* the aroma of coffee *and* where he was on the coastline, all at the same time.

Think about your own sport. Where do you need to flex your attention?

For example, if you play a ball or racket sport such as netball, squash or volleyball, you need to focus on your opponent's movement and the ball. Maybe you're a road cyclist, where attention to a breakaway from another rider needs to be held along with a focus on the terrain ahead. Perhaps you do weightlifting and need to shift attention between the flow of the lift, your grip and posture. Or in golf where the focus pivots between the hole and the ball.

Whatever your sport, a constant switch in attention is often required. The danger is we either snap out of the present moment as we make that switch or get stuck focussing on one aspect, caught up in our thoughts and totally lose sight of other aspects. And that's when our performance can dip.

We have one last exercise to help you develop a more flexible approach to playing in the now.

Flexing your attention[7]

Set a timer for two minutes. Focus your attention on the sole of your left foot. Notice what it feels like. Notice the sensations there. Notice how warm or cold it is. Notice how the skin feels. Notice the amount of space your left foot takes. Notice if your attention wanders off, and if it does, gently bring it back to focus on the sole of your left foot. Keep your focus on that until the timer rings.

Pause for a moment and reflect. Likely your mind will have wandered and you had to bring it back to focus on the sole of your foot again. And maybe you noticed some things you don't normally notice about your left sole – the shape, an itchy feeling, a difference in the warmth of your heel and your toes and so on.

Now reset the timer for a further two minutes. Only this time do the same with the sole of your right foot. Really notice the sensations and observations. And if your mind wanders off, simply bring it back.

If you are like us, you might have noticed different things. Perhaps it felt like the time passed slowly? Did your Thinking Mind tell you there was nothing new to learn?

Now set the timer one final time, for another two minutes. Only this time, see if you can be aware of both your left sole and your right sole at the same time. Try not to alternate your focus, but instead broaden the beam of your attention to allow you to focus on both simultaneously. Again, if your mind wanders away, gently direct it back to the practice. Do this until the timer pings.

Was that hard? Did you find yourself noticing one foot and then the other? Could you notice both? And did your awareness come and go?

This exercise builds your capability to flex your attention when you need to – whether it's in the middle of game play, when you've been listening to the coach and now need to focus on the game, or in the jostling of a long-distance race when you need to refocus on your tactics. You are learning how to ground your awareness, using the soles of your feet as a reference point. If you find yourself caught up in your head, bringing your attention back to both feet at the same time gives you a small window of opportunity to decide what to do next (instead of responding mindlessly) and also helps you to learn how to flex your attention.

In his book, tennis star Novak Djokovic talks about how mindfulness and meditation have transformed his game.[8] He explains how he has incorporated aspects of meditation into his daily routines, to help him not only in his tennis career but also in his day-to-day life. In particular, he references breathing and mindfulness as a way to switch off from technologies and distractions and to help him maintain his energy and concentration on court.

Practising mindfulness makes you better at flexing and focussing your attention.[9]

Think of it like training Matty

Learning how to *Play in the Now* is a lot like training Jenna's puppy, Matty. We both agree he's adorable. And if you take Matty for a walk and bring his favourite ball with you, Matty will dash around excitedly, picking up the ball, putting it down, picking it up again, running in a circle and then bringing the ball back and dropping it at your feet. He'll very happily play with the ball. At least that is until something or someone exciting catches his eye. He is easily distracted. Then the ball is dropped, forgotten, as Matty runs off exploring a tree, a bench, even a blade of grass. He turns his focus to whatever grabs his attention next and needs Jenna's help to remember that he had a ball just a few moments ago. With that reminder, he can concentrate on using his keen senses to find it again. And Jenna does this over and over again with Matty, as he learns to be more attentive and focussed.

Developing your focus and concentration using mindfulness is like training and playing with a puppy (who is all over the place and wandering off everywhere!). Mindfulness takes practice. Here are a few things you can do:

- Teach your mind by being gentle and patient, kind and persistent – guide your mind back to the present

- Be active and alert – keep in the right now (rather than doze off … it's not a relaxation practice)

- Don't try to control your mind – you are not trying to get rid of all your unpleasant or stressful feelings, just to notice them

- Choose how you respond – you are not trying to achieve anything, just be aware of the present moment.

What's in your kitbag?

Here's what's gone into your kitbag from this chapter.

You now know your Thinking Mind is going to wander in all sorts of directions, thinking, planning, problem-solving and analysing. Whilst it's doing this to try and protect you, the end result is you get caught up in unhelpful stories about your capability as an athlete that limit your options and your potential. That's why you've learnt to mindfully *Play in the Now*.

Mindfulness is about using your Observing Mind to notice these thoughts and feelings, bringing your attention back to the present moment. You've practised how to use an anchor, such as a sip of water or your breath to connect with the here and now. An anchor is something you can return to when your mind wanders off. An effective anchor will be different depending on your sport and can be internal or external to you.

By strengthening your ability to *Play in the Now*, you can focus on what's important to you rather than get caught up worrying about past mistakes or future situations. You have built your awareness of your internal thoughts and feelings, whilst also paying attention to whatever tasks you're engaged in.

Mindfully staying in the present with a flexible and focussed attention gives you the option to make more effective choices about how you train and compete. That way you can bring your best possible performance each and every time.

You'll need your Observing Mind and your *Play in the Now* skills for Chapter 3. Here you'll begin to *Drop the Struggle* with your unhelpful thoughts and feelings.

Chapter 3

Drop the struggle with your thoughts

When I stop struggling, I float. It's the law.
ANON

Professional golfer Rory McIlroy was at the top of his game in 2011, performing brilliantly in The Masters, one of golf's biggest tournaments. He was playing some of his best-ever golf and going into the final round; he was four shots ahead of the rest of the field. His round got off to a shaky start, but the 10th hole is where it all started to go wrong for McIlroy.

He started to listen to the doubts. He let the voice in his head that told him not to crumble consume him. His mind was overthinking each shot, and he found it hard to deal with the uncomfortableness of the situation.[1] McIlroy went triple bogey, bogey, double bogey over that three-hole stretch as a chance at victory ebbed away from him. He finished with the worst final-round score in Masters history at an eight-over par.

Success was within his reach, but critical thoughts took over and snatched it from him in the cruellest of fashions.

Whilst most of us don't get to compete on the world stage and have a chance of winning golf's biggest tournament, being beset by unhelpful thoughts is something we will all have experienced. How do you deal with this? How can you prevent them from ruining your performance, your life? These are questions we will explore in this chapter.

What are thoughts?

We have thousands of them each and every day, but have you ever actually stopped to think about what thoughts are?

It is an incredibly difficult question to answer. Scientists have long explored thoughts from a neuroscientific point of view. What specific brain networks are involved? Is it the firing of neurons that produces thought? Are conscious thoughts different from subconscious ones? Many questions, but at this stage of scientific understanding, not too many answers.

Instead of getting too much into the science, we like to describe thoughts as images, pictures, memories or stories passing through our mind. They are usually short-lived, meaning they don't hang around for long, and we now know we actually have very little control over them.

We can be aware of thoughts, clearly identify them and speak about them to others. But also we can be unaware of thoughts, totally caught up in something else and not aware of what's passing through our mind at any one time.

The complex level of thought that we experience and our ability to articulate our thoughts via language separate us from other species on this planet. Thoughts help us to plan, organise and make decisions about the future. We clearly couldn't play sports without them, so there's no doubt they are very helpful for our life, performance and sense of happiness.

However, there is one key problem that grips humans today. This is the tendency we have to believe all of our thoughts. Although you may not have known it, this is probably one of the main reasons that you picked up this book.

Of course, thoughts can be truthful, realistic, honest and wise, but it's important to realise they aren't always. Often our thoughts will deceive us with false narratives based on our fears and insecurities. That's why, if we believe them fully, they become problematic and impact our ability to perform both in life and in sport.

Let's take the example of Aneka – a diver about to take a winning, or losing, dive. As she steps up to the board, a thought pops into her mind – 'I bet you're going to over extend'. Unfortunate timing to have that kind of thought, and definitely not one she wants at that moment. There are two important questions to consider here:

Can she get rid of this thought? We know the answer to that is no. There is very little point in her trying to suppress it; in fact, that is likely to make it worse.

Does she have to let it rule her actions? The answer to this question is also no. As she steps up to take the dive, she has two choices. To take that thought seriously, believe it to be true and act in line with it. As a result, of course, her entry into the water has a good chance of being far from vertical. 'See' she says 'I knew it'.

The other choice, as she steps up to the board, is to recognise the thought is there, but choose not to allow it to dictate her actions. She could complete her pre-dive routine as normal, take a deep breath, laugh to herself that her mind is trying to sabotage things again and step up confidently to the dive. 'Keep my head still, take a smooth approach' she says to herself, and she makes a clean entry into the water.

You can have the same unhelpful thought, but by responding to it in different ways, you'll create very different outcomes.

You will be able to think of lots of examples in your own life and sport, where your mind tells you something that you have, in the past, believed to be true and allowed to guide your actions. Take a few moments to make a note of some of these:

Is it true?

Note down the times when you believed a thought to be true and it impacted your actions.

Dropping the struggle

Getting caught up in your thoughts and believing them all to be true is what psychologists call 'fusion'. This happens when we only use our Thinking Mind and don't use our Observing Mind.

Imagine that your hands are your thoughts.[2] Hold your hands together, palms open, as if they are the pages of an open book. Slowly raise your hands towards your face until they are covering your eyes. Take a few seconds to look at the world around you through the gaps between your fingers and notice how this affects your view.

What would it be like going around all day with your hands covering your eyes in this manner? How would it limit you? How much would you miss? How would it reduce your ability to respond to the world around you?

This is like fusion. We become so caught up in our thoughts that we lose contact with many aspects of our here-and-now experience, and our thoughts have such a huge influence over what we do, that our ability to act effectively is significantly reduced.

The opposite to this – what's known as defusion – is when you are able to step back from your thoughts and see them as just images and stories passing through your mind, rather than the absolute truth. It's the opposite of getting tangled in your thoughts and believing everything they tell you. Defusion means to 'step back' and separate or detach from our thoughts.[3] It's also known as unhooking, literally 'unfastening yourself from something'. You can gain a sense of perspective and choose the thoughts you want to listen to and guide your actions, and the ones you want to just let pass by. This is what we refer to as *Drop the Struggle.*

> Cover your eyes again with your hands, and this time slowly lower your hands. As your hands descend beneath your eyes, notice how much easier it is to connect with others and the world around you. This is how you *Drop the Struggle.* As you lower your hands, your thoughts do not disappear. Lay your hands on your lap. They are still there, but getting some separation allows you to engage more flexibly, freeing you to choose to act in ways that are important to you.

Notice that we are not asking you to replace negative thoughts with positive ones. Whilst that can be helpful, it requires a lot of mental energy and is hard to maintain over the long term. You don't have to think endless positive thoughts to perform well or be happy, you just have to *Drop the Struggle* with the ones that are holding you back.

When we are caught up in the struggle	When we drop the struggle
Thoughts are reality; what we're thinking is actually present, here and now.	Thoughts are merely sounds, words, stories and bits of language passing through our heads.
Thoughts are the truth; we literally believe every thought that pops into our mind.	Thoughts may or may not be true. We don't need to automatically believe them.
Thoughts are important; we take them seriously and give them our full attention.	Thoughts may or may not be important. We can pay attention only if they're helpful.
Thoughts are orders; we automatically obey them.	Thoughts are not orders. We don't have to obey them.
Thoughts are wise; we assume they know best and we follow their advice.	Thoughts may or may not be wise. We don't have to automatically follow their advice.

The thoughts we have are nothing more than words and pictures. We don't need to let them pull us around or dictate the things we do; otherwise, they can stop us from living the life we want and achieving our goals. Knowing this can liberate you from so much psychological and emotional pain and have a transformative effect on your sport and life.

Olivia is a competitive 26-year-old table-tennis player. Olivia struggled with unhelpful thoughts. Especially if her opponent was a player she knew and had beaten before, her mind would go over and over thoughts like 'everyone is expecting you to win', 'this should be easy, don't make it hard work for yourself', 'I can't believe you just hit that in the net, it was the easiest shot on earth'. On and on her chatty mind would go.

Olivia tried many tactics over the years to block out these thoughts. She would try to push them away, have a distraction phrase like 'Keep going you've got this' and even put an elastic band on her wrist which she used to try and help her 'snap out' of these thoughts. Alas, no matter how hard she tried, those pesky thoughts kept coming back and throughout the match they would only get louder and stronger and more debilitating to her performance.

After learning about dropping the struggle, Olivia then decided to change her mental approach. She was doubtful it would have any effect, but what she had been trying for years wasn't working anyway so she figured she might as well give it a go. Olivia changed her whole mindset. Instead of trying to get rid of the unhelpful thoughts she was having, she realised she could just *Drop the Struggle* with them. It became irrelevant whether she had the unhelpful thoughts or not. She learnt to get perspective on her thoughts, not let them rule her game and even make a joke of them rather than taking them so seriously. It transformed her game beyond recognition; not only did her performances improve dramatically, but she actually started to enjoy games rather than wishing they were over. Olivia reflected on the transformation: 'I realised that it doesn't matter what your mind says when you're on court, what matters is how you choose to respond to it. I went from letting my thoughts dictate my actions, to letting me decide how I wanted to play'.

Getting better at dropping the struggle

Knowing how to *Drop the Struggle* with your thoughts – being able to step back and watch them, rather than getting caught up in them, is the most powerful mindset technique you can have. It can totally transform your life and your sporting performance. But it's not easy, and you might well be reading this thinking, 'well that sounds great, but how do I actually do it? How do I step back and use my Observing Mind to help me decide which thoughts I want to listen to and guide my actions?'

This is where defusion exercises come in. Just like you would go for a run to improve cardio fitness, you also need to work on your ability to *Drop the Struggle* with your thoughts. It doesn't just happen by reading, there has to be 'doing' as well. Here are some exercises that will help this become a habitual part of the way you think. It can often be helpful to first practise these away from the intensity of the sports arena whilst you get used to this way of thinking. Pick out one or two that you think will work best for you in the circumstances you face and try to incorporate them into your life as much as possible.

It's intense and I need a quick strategy

Use this exercise when you're in a stressful or intense situation and need a quick strategy to help you, fast!

Lemon, Lemon, Lemon[4]

Start off by thinking about a lemon. Take a minute or two to really bring the image of a lemon into your mind.

What thoughts do you have? What images come to mind? What's the colour and texture of the skin and the flesh? What can you smell? How does it taste in your mouth?

Now are there any lemons in the room with you? Probably not. Yet simply because you thought of a 'lemon' you can – to some extent – see, feel, smell and taste it. You may even have had a very real reaction at the thought of biting into the flesh and getting that sharp bitter taste on your tongue.

Our mind is so good at interpreting our thoughts that it brings a whole lot more to the table than just the specific words themselves. We begin to think that our thoughts are real and concrete.

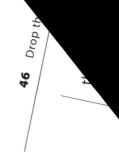

Next, repeat the word 'lemon' out loud as fast as
30 seconds. Give it a try. Lemon, lemon, lemon
… say it louder!

What did you notice? What happened to the ..

Often what we experience is that the word becomes a bunch of jumbled, silly sounds. You maybe even found yourself laughing a bit. Or maybe the word stayed intact but lost its meaning.

This is the thing about thoughts – they are just words!

This is an exercise you can practise with any thoughts that are familiar to you and your mind (e.g. fat, useless, failure) and that you get caught up in. Whatever the thought is, just repeat it to yourself over and over until it becomes meaningless and a jumble of sounds. Over time you'll learn not to take it quite so seriously, and maybe even laugh at it.

Give it a go, be curious and notice what happens. Make a note of how and where you might use this activity.

The same thoughts keep cropping up

It may be that your mind has a favourite 'story' it often tells you, particularly when you are doing something challenging. Use this exercise when you recognise similar thoughts cropping up again and again.

Story time

Humans love hearing stories. Right from childhood, we learn to engross ourselves in a fairy tale or made-up story, and we begin to develop the ability ourselves to create stories in our own minds. Remember the ones you told when you were younger about the monster under the bed, or the fortress in the woods hat the king used for battles. Into adulthood, we still tell stories to our friends and family, often using humour, exaggeration or twists for effect. We also learn to tell ourselves stories. We have a constant narrative in our heads telling us about our own lives and how good, or not, we think we are. You will have certain stories that your mind likes to repeat to you.

What are they? Have a think, and identify your Thinking Mind's most deeply entrenched stories. They could be pleasant ones about you or your life, but quite often they are harsh and critical ones about what you can't do, or how you aren't good enough.

Perhaps when stepping up to take a penalty, your mind starts going on about the fact that you never score penalties or that your family will be so embarrassed if you miss. Or if you're feeling under the weather and questioning whether you should train or not, your mind goes on about how lazy you are or that you always back out at the first opportunity.

Once you've identified them, the next step is to give them names, such as the 'loser' story, or 'you're going to mess up again' story, or 'I can't do it' story. Often there will be several variations on a theme.

When your stories show up, acknowledge them by name. For example, you could say to yourself, 'Ah yes. I recognise this. That old favourite, the "I'm a failure" story'. Or 'Aha! Here comes the "I can't cope" story'.

Once you've acknowledged a story, that's it – just let it be. You don't have to challenge it or push it away, nor do you have to give it much attention. Simply let it come and go as it pleases, whilst you channel your energy into doing something you value.

If you find it hard to think of stories right now, watch out for them in the next few days and weeks. Look out for the narratives that crop up time after time.

My self-critical thoughts get me down

This exercise is extremely effective when you're finding self-critical thoughts get you down. Use it when thoughts are in the form of 'I am …'

I'm having the thought that[5]

To begin this exercise, first bring to mind an upsetting thought that takes the form 'I am X'. For example, 'I'm not good enough'. Preferably pick a thought that recurs frequently and that often bothers you or stops you from performing at your best.

Now focus on that thought and believe it as much as you can for ten seconds.

Next, take that thought and, in front of it, insert this phrase: 'I'm having the thought that …'. Play that thought again, but this time with the phrase attached. Think to yourself, 'I'm having the thought that I am X'. Notice what happens.

Now do that again, but this time the phrase is slightly longer: 'I notice I'm having the thought that …'. Think to yourself, 'I notice I'm having the thought that I am X'. Notice what happens.

You may notice that your mind tries to respond with … 'But it's true' and continues to give you reasons why. If that happens, that's ok. Remember our minds are reason-giving machines. The goal of the exercise is not to get rid of the thought, but to stop arguing with it. When you are noticing your thoughts, you are using your Observing Mind. This helps to create space between the thought and you. And in that space, the thought starts to lose power and you have more capacity to focus on the present moment and take action towards the person you want to be, not the one your mind is currently telling you that you are. Notice that you haven't got rid of the thought, it hasn't gone away, but it has less of a negative impact on what you do.

Practising this exercise allows you to look *at* your thoughts, rather than *from* your thoughts. When you notice thoughts, rather than being caught up in them, you can see these thoughts as what they are, not as what they seem to be. You have more opportunities to make a choice about what to do next.

I am trying to prove my thoughts are/are not true

Sometimes you find yourself fighting with your Thinking Mind and using lots of energy trying to prove that your thoughts are either true or false. This exercise is brilliant for helping you to loosen your grip on this battle and take your focus back to playing your sport.

Newspaper headlines

When we read about well-known athletes in the tabloids, we know that many of the headlines and content are false or misleading. Some are exaggerated for effect, others are made up entirely. Some are true.

Let's take Serena Williams as an example. A world-famous tennis player, she has lots of articles written about her – some good, some bad. Now, she has a choice. In scenario one, she gets very upset about these articles. She reads them again and again, dwells on them for days and rants and rages to her team about what the papers are saying about her. Perhaps she even attempts to lodge a lawsuit (which is stressful and eats up a lot of time, energy and money). She doesn't seem to be able to move on from them, and it impacts her tennis and her relationships in and away from the sport.

In scenario two, she takes this all in her stride; accepts it as part of being famous and doesn't let it get to her. When she sees the headlines about herself, she just shrugs it off. She doesn't try to get rid of every single newspaper that has printed a story, and she doesn't waste her time reading, analysing and discussing them. She doesn't expend energy trying to prove if what the paper is printing is true or false. As a result of this approach, her tennis performance remains at the highest standards, and she is able to continue her work with a lot less struggle.

Same scenario – two different approaches and two very different outcomes.

What are some of the negative headlines your Thinking Mind broadcasts about you? Use your imagination to place them as a newspaper headline, perhaps with a picture and a quote. Imagine spotting this newspaper as you walk past a copy in the street. You take a sideways glance as you go by, but don't stop to pick it up or read it in detail. You know it's there and you're not trying to change it, but neither are you wasting precious time, energy and mental resources focussing on it.

The beauty of this exercise is you have the choice to *Drop the Struggle.* There's no need for your mind to be caught up in the ping-pong between 'It's true I am …' and 'That's such a lie, I am …' and so on – you can fill in the blanks here for yourself. It frees you up to get on with being an athlete.

What's in your kitbag?

The kitbag for this chapter contains one big idea: You don't have to think endless positive thoughts to perform well or be happy. Your mind thinks all manner of thoughts and will wander in all sorts of directions. But the amazing thing is, you are not your thoughts and you don't have to believe everything they tell you. You don't need to let them push you around or dictate the things you do; otherwise, they can stop you from being the athlete and person you want to be.

You can use the exercises in this chapter to help you *Drop the Struggle* with your thoughts and feelings. You'll be letting them go instead of being caught up in them, so you can take action on what matters to you instead.

Now you're starting to develop the tools to stop getting caught up in your thoughts and feelings; in Chapter 4 we'll unpick how we respond when we don't want to have certain thoughts. Instead of fighting them all the time, you'll learn how to make space for them. We'll call it learning to *Accept Being Uncomfortable.*

Chapter 4

Accept being uncomfortable

*It's pretty well impossible to create a better life if you're
not prepared to have some uncomfortable feelings.*
RUSS HARRIS, HAPPINESS TRAP

As an athlete, you have chosen to put yourself under pressure. Whether you like it or not, it is a part of training to be your best and competing against others. Whilst there can be negative effects of pressure, it's something that can also help us improve our performance and learn new things. Although the feeling of being under pressure may seem unwanted, it's actually our response to pressure that's the problem.

We all face pressure

Sometimes pressure gets a bad reputation. Maybe you have thoughts like these – 'Oh I always crumble when things get tough', 'I'm too scared to face the pressure of playing against Samira' or 'I don't like competing, it's too much to face'.

Will Greenwood explained his battle with pressure in the few days before England's historic 2003 Rugby World Cup final win:

> On Wednesday, Thursday, Oh my God, don't mess this up! Left on my own with demons, thoughts, utter fear. The only way I could quieten the tannoy is if I'm sleeping … Friday, pushing the food around the plate, feeling physically sick, thinking 'I can't do this, I can't do this, I can't do this', emotional energy spent. Saturday morning 'Oh it's game day!' Saturday afternoon, 'I'm back in it. I'm alright'.[1]

And it's not without justification. For example, take those pressure moments in basketball when the shot needs to go in. Evidence shows that in the last 30 seconds of tight basketball games, players in the women's and men's professional leagues in North America are 5.8% and 3.1% respectively less likely to score from a free throw, than at other moments in the game. Pressure can get to us.

We feel pressure when the demands of a situation exceed our real or perceived ability to cope with them. Our experience of pressure shows up in several ways – in our bodies, our thoughts and our emotions. And the same situation may produce different responses between you and your teammates, or on different occasions.

Where pressure shows up

Let's start to examine where and how pressure shows up for you. Think back to the last week or month:

Identify one situation where you felt pressure...
What was it about this situation that made you feel pressured? ....
What thoughts showed up in your mind? ....
What sensations showed up in your body?..
What emotions were you aware of feeling?..

Often we forget we are in these 'pressure situations' by choice. We get so caught up in our worries and anxieties that we fail to be in the moment and rush mindlessly through competition and practice. Gareth Southgate, as manager of the England men's football team, reflected on how pressure impacted him as a player. In his biography, reliving the sudden death penalty shootout against Germany in Euro 96, he said 'All I wanted was the ball: put it on the spot, get it over and done with'.[2] Southgate famously crumbled under the pressure, not wanting to pause in the uncomfortableness of the moment. Unsurprisingly, he missed that crucial shot.

We hate the feeling of nerves and anxiety that pressure creates. Our minds can convince us that we want to get out of these situations, and question 'Why do we do this to ourselves?' Instead of feeling motivated to achieve our goal, we spend our time worrying about what might happen and run through all the different ways that we might fail or mess up.

The relationship between pressure and performance

The thing is, pressure can be a good thing and can actually help us perform at our best. Here's how this looks visually:[3]

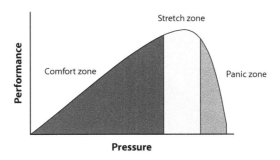

We call this the pressure performance curve. As the pressure we face increases, so can our performance, until we hit a peak of performance. Beyond this, increases in pressure cause our performance to drop away.

As individuals, we have different natural preferences along this curve.

Perhaps you prefer to be on the left-hand side, firmly in your comfort zone. This is a safe place to go back to, especially when things get challenging. Being in your comfort zone is like being in the safety of your own house, you don't have to go outside and speak to anyone, you know where everything is and can have it just as you like it. In sport this might mean you fear trying new things, you don't push yourself in training sessions, or you stay playing in the same team even when you dream of moving on.

Alternatively, your natural tendencies might lead you more towards the panic zone. You push it hard a lot of the time. You commit to too many things, you rush about, going from one thing to the next without any time to pause, take a breath and chill out. You're so scared of quiet time, or being on your own, that you avoid it altogether. On the sports pitch, we'd spot you training seven days a week when the programme says five days, playing mindlessly on court or rushing to learn new skills when you hadn't mastered the basics yet.

Both these types of behaviours are what we call avoidant. Avoidance is defined as the ongoing struggle to avoid, suppress or get rid of unwanted thoughts, feelings or memories.[4] You can see how these behaviours link to the pressure performance curve.

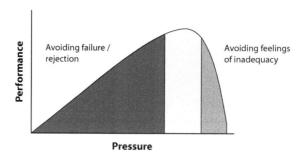

Towards the left-hand side, you are likely avoiding the thoughts and feelings of failure or being dismissed by someone. Towards the right-hand side, you are likely overcompensating for feelings or thoughts of inadequacy or having to prove yourself.

Perhaps you're prepared to be in the stretch zone and are willing to accept that you may face some uncomfortable thoughts and feelings there. The stretch zone is where growth thrives and performance often improves. We'd see you at training and in competition focussed on doing the things that are important for your performance, learning new things even if that means being prepared to fail and connecting with others around you. You are prepared to accept the uncomfortable feelings of being in the stretch zone.

An example of an athlete willing to be in the stretch zone is Jessica Ennis-Hill, the British heptathlete.

Going into her first Olympic Games, Ennis-Hill suffered an injury in her right foot – the foot she used for take-off in the long jump. During her recovery, she and her coach recognised that the load going through her foot could be too much for it to take. Ennis-Hill decided to stretch herself outside of her comfort zone – what she had known since the beginning – and do something different in an attempt to keep fit and deliver a world-class performance. Even though it might not work, she changed her take-off leg and started jumping off her left leg. This meant building strength in a different way, along with re-learning the technique of flying through the air on the other side. It was a big decision, one that could be career-changing for her. And indeed it was – in her first event after the injury she recorded her best-ever score.

Ennis-Hill could have stayed with what she knew and hoped for the best. Instead, she challenged herself to do something completely different, manage the psychological uncertainty that came with that and went on to achieve great things in many world championships and Olympic Games.[5]

The challenge is to be able to find and stay in the stretch zone. Of course, you are just human and if you push yourself too hard, too often, you will likely reach burnout or panic, or a complete loss of motivation. But don't let your fears and doubts hold you back. If you're not prepared to feel at least a little bit uncomfortable, you won't know what you are truly capable of.

Our response to pressure is the problem

Whilst we know that pressure can have a negative impact on performance, we also know that pressure can often be a really good thing for performance. We see that personal bests are created and records are broken in competition, because pressure can bring out the best in people, *if* they embrace it. For example, across a range of sports, some 20 world records were notched up in the very pressurised environment of the Tokyo 2020 Olympics.[6]

Pressure itself isn't a bad thing; it's our reaction to it that can be. Let's take a look at a few examples.

- **Sometimes we believe our response to pressure is pre-programmed.** We say things like, 'All my family crumble under pressure, so that's why I get nervous before a race' or 'There's no way I could take the pressure of playing in the cup, I always struggle'. When actually, although our genetic makeup might make us predisposed to deal with pressure in certain ways, or to be more anxious,[7] our response is much more down to our learnt behaviour than our genetics. And the good news is this means we can change it.

- **Every so often the feelings of pressure seem too intense.** Our feelings can seem overwhelming. Earlier in this book we learnt how our brain has evolved with a fight, flight and freeze response system. This is all that's happening when under pressure – you have an important situation ahead of you, and your body is getting ready. Now you might be faced with a real threat or risk of harm. This might include combat situations or a risk of accidents where your life is under threat and those danger signals are important to keep you safe. But in most sports situations, the strong thoughts and feelings that come up for us – be they butterflies in our stomach, a wave of anxiety in our chest or the thought that we will be humiliated – are not a barrier between you and good performance. It's when we interpret that as a bad thing that it starts to have a negative impact.

- **We believe that feeling pressure is a sign of weakness**. Maybe ask yourself, 'Do I think being anxious before an important event in my sporting year means I have a personality defect, or I am not cut out for it, or even that I lack motivation?' When we buy into these ideas, it's all too easy to look across at our teammate or our closest rival, imagine that they never struggle with pressure and think there must be something wrong with us. Whereas the truth is we all feel pressure and nerves at some point in our sports careers. Being selected, stepping up to an important competition, facing the next test; that person next to you is probably feeling worried or anxious too. The difference is, they are not focussing their energy on trying to fight those feelings.

- **Finally, we can succumb to the social expectation that to be good at sport, we should always feel good too.** Take for example some of the physical symptoms we experience when we are feeling the pressure – increased heart rate, sweaty palms, butterflies in our stomachs. What often happens is we experience these symptoms and interpret them as negative. 'Oh dear, that means I'm nervous and I won't perform well today'. But these are simply physical responses that help you prepare

for what you're about to do. Even though we'd like to, we can't –
and don't need to – feel good all of the time.

Take a good look at these examples. If none of them ring true to you,
you are happy facing into pressure, going with the feelings that come
up and never avoiding people or situations that cause you stress, you
are starting from a great place. It may be that you think you have all the
strategies you need to deal with pressure and nerves. Even so, we'd still
encourage you to read, and answer honestly, the five questions in the
next section. You may surprise yourself.

Are you willing to do something different?

Of course, it's good practice to look at proactive ways that can reduce
pressure. Making sure you are prepared, doing your homework on the
competition, having a race plan, connecting with teammates, following
the training programme, scouting the venue, reducing sessions when
you need to meet a work/school deadline … There are many ways to
ensure that unnecessary pressure is minimised as you play your sport.

But if you are looking to improve your skills and performance, pressure is inevitable (and as we've learnt, often helpful). Let's see what
you've tried to get rid of the uncomfortable thoughts and feelings that
come up and look at how they work in the long term.

Doing something different

1. **What have you tried?**

Think of the main thoughts, feelings, emotions, memories and
urges that you do not want. Maybe you do your best not to feel
nervous before a big event or attempt to stop worrying about
an important result. Perhaps you do your utmost to avoid feeling
sad, anxious or frustrated. It's likely you try to ignore them, find

ways of distracting yourself from how you are feeling or cover them up with other positive emotions to give you a temporary sense of feeling good.

What sort of things have you tried to do or use to get rid of them?[8]

Distraction: what do you do to distract yourself from, or take your mind off painful thoughts and feelings? For example, keep busy, over-train, eat food, surf social media.

Opting out: what important, meaningful activities, challenges or people do you avoid or quit? For example, not entering a race, quitting a training session, feigning injury, sitting on the sidelines instead of with the team. Of course, if they're not important, meaningful or life-enhancing, then opting out is no problem!

Thinking strategies: how do you try (consciously or not) to think your way out of feeling uncomfortable? For example, worrying, dwelling on the past, fantasising about the future, thinking 'It's not fair …' or 'If only …', blaming yourself, others or the world, criticising yourself, judging yourself, analysing yourself or the situation? Or maybe you have tried some typical sport psychology practices such as talking logically and rationally to yourself, positive thinking, positive affirmations, planning, constructive problem-solving, making To Do lists, repeating inspirational sayings or proverbs or challenging or disputing negative thoughts?

Substances and other strategies: what substances do you use or put into your body to avoid or get rid of difficult feelings?

Do you use any other strategies to get rid of or avoid these feelings, For example, yoga, picking fights, dancing, music, self-harming, smashing things, staying in bed …?

2. **How well has that worked?**

Let's now take a look at each of the things you've tried and ask yourself :

- How many of these give you some short-term relief? How long does that relief last?
- In the long term, has anything you've tried gotten rid of the feelings that you don't want, so they never come back?

3. **What has that cost you?**

If you've become over-reliant on these methods, and not used them flexibly, what have they cost you in terms of missed opportunities, energy, team relationships, impact on fitness and so on? Maybe you've pulled out of a race, not played your best or damaged a relationship with someone?

4. **What's that been like for you?**

So you've put lots of effort into getting rid of those pesky thoughts and feelings. And you've found many ways to get short-term relief but in the long run you still struggle when faced with pressure, it never goes away. We imagine that feels tough. Really tough. And know that what you've tried makes perfect sense; it's what we all try to do, so you can be kind to yourself here.

5. **Are you open to something different?**

If you've been fighting your ability to manage pressure in sport, despite trying hard, it still doesn't get any easier and it's taken a toll on you, are you open to trying something different?

The struggle switch

If you are still reading, we assume you are open to a new way of dealing with pressure. And you now know that it's not the pressure that's the problem, it's our reaction to it. So let's find a helpful way to think about our reaction.

Imagine that you have a struggle switch in your mind.[9] As you start to feel some of the symptoms of pressure, instead of recognising that these are normal, natural feelings that mean you are ready, and motivated to do well, you panic and the struggle switch flicks on. When the struggle switch is on, your feelings of worry become even stronger as you desperately try to get rid of them. They then have even more influence over you than they did before, causing heightened negativity about what you're feeling. In this state, it's no wonder you are unable to perform at your best!

Now imagine that you start to experience some of the physical sensations of pressure, but this time your struggle switch stays off. It's not that you like those feelings or want them, it's just that you don't struggle with them. You don't invest your time and energy in getting rid of those emotions (an impossible task as we now know). Instead you invest your time and energy in things that are going to help you perform at your best.

You can't get rid of those feelings that come with pressure; but by keeping the struggle switch off, they don't have to dominate your thoughts and have a negative impact on your performance.

Saying yes to your feelings

It's scary out there in the stretch zone. All sorts of difficult thoughts and feelings arise when you challenge yourself and step into the unknown. We've discovered we don't need to get rid of negative feelings to improve our performance. Thankfully there is an alternative – an even better way of dealing with difficult thoughts and feelings that we experience when we step outside of our comfort zone. This method requires a lot less energy than trying to get rid of them, and is a lot more effective!

The technical term for keeping this struggle switch off is *acceptance*.

Acceptance literally means 'taking what is offered', whether it's uncomfortable or not.

Let's explore this. Imagine you have an important competition coming up, something big.[10] You get up and have some breakfast, but realise you've dawdled and now you are late. There's no time to waste. You rush upstairs and put your kit on. You run to the bathroom. Just enough time to clean your teeth, put your trainers on and catch your bus. Halfway to the bathroom, you realise you've put on that annoying sock, the one with the loose elastic that won't stay up. Aargh. Your mind fills with thoughts about how gross it feels when your sock wrinkles up and falls down near your heel. You can feel the frustration rising up your chest. You stop, grab your sock and yank it back up your foot. No time to go back and find another sock or you'll miss your bus.

You run downstairs and get to the front door, and the sock is wrinkled up under your heel again, leaving half your foot bare in your trainer. Argh. You stop in your tracks and pull it up, lacing your trainers more tightly, saying to yourself, 'that will keep it in place!' You grab your kitbag and run out of the door.

Of course, this doesn't work and within a few strides the sock is lumpy under your foot again. You can't bear the feeling as with every step it scratches the sole of your foot. You reach down, pull your trainer off and pull the sock up again, only this time your kitbag swings off your shoulder and lands upside down on the floor, the contents spilling onto the pavement. You look up to see your bus go speeding past. And your sock is still wrinkled under your foot.

That seems like a pretty rubbish start to the day. What would you say is the cause of the bad morning?

You might say that the sock was the cause of the bad morning. After all, it kept falling down and that made you have to keep yanking it up? You might also be berating yourself for the fact you didn't get up earlier, or have a spare pair of socks in your kitbag.

But what if the sock getting wrinkled was something you couldn't control, something that was going to happen unexpectedly or repeatedly, like having feelings? Might you be better off leaving your sock wrinkled?

Learning to *Accept Being Uncomfortable* is a difficult skill to master. This is because acceptance isn't distraction, it's not ignoring and it's not repressing – things we are all pretty good at. Acceptance is being willing to wear the wrinkled sock, even though you don't like the feeling of it being bunched up under your foot. In the sports arena, it's being willing to be nervous, to feel anxious and to fear what will happen if you lose. But to go for it anyway because it's something that is important to you and something you want to do in your life. Accepting doesn't mean giving up or admitting defeat. Neither does it mean just gritting your teeth and bearing it. It also doesn't mean that you necessarily want those feelings. It just means fully opening yourself to what is happening in your mind right now – whether that is good or bad – and continuing to do your sport in the way that you have trained and you know you can.

The wrinkled sock exercise

If you have your own wrinkled sock that often falls down, try to wear it for a while and let it slip down. Or you could try slipping some crinkled tissue in your trainer or a tiny stone. Walk around and allow whatever thoughts, feelings, sensations and urges to show up, along with the wrinkled sock, tissue or pebble, whilst you go and do something that matters to you.

What did you notice about that experience?

Approaching your feelings like you might the sock, just letting them be, will help you to be more willing to have them.

Acceptance is ...	Acceptance isn't ...
A wilful act – a choice	Giving up or admitting defeat
Acknowledgement of what exists	Gritting your teeth and bearing it
Being open to what is happening	Wanting or choosing to feel bad or negative
An active process, one that must be practised consciously	Passive. It doesn't mean that you can't work on changing things
Something that can be practised in all areas of life ... current experience, others' opinions, your appearance, your emotions and so on	Judging something as good or bad, pleasant or unpleasant, it's simply acknowledging it as being present

The reason acceptance and turning the struggle switch off is so important is because many of the things we value most – in life and in sport – bring pressure and with pressure comes a whole range of feelings, both pleasant and unpleasant. Actively choosing to enter a competition will probably bring about a feeling of nerves; competing against someone better than us will most likely cause us to feel anxious; and going to a trial, by nature, means you might not get selected and consequently feel sadness, embarrassment, disappointment or frustration. When these thoughts or feelings do arise, we either waste all our energy doing our best to get rid of them or we avoid the pressure situation in our sport up front. Either way, we are limiting our potential as an athlete.

But what if you just accepted them all? If you say 'Ok, the feelings I don't like have arrived.' You let them in and choose to spend more time focussing on the helpful ones. The unhelpful ones will soon quieten down anyway.

Eventually, you may learn to actually welcome uncomfortable or difficult feelings such as fear or anxiety, because you know that when handled well, they can lead you to the highest heights of your performance.

> Practising acceptance brings results. International-level chess players[11] who were trained to accept difficult thoughts and feelings and unhook from them improved their performance, compared with chess players who had not received this training. In addition, the training helped them to significantly reduce how much they believed unpleasant thoughts, sensations and feelings during competitions. It also reduced the number of unhelpful reactions they had to their thoughts and feelings.

Sometimes learning to *Accept Being Uncomfortable* is easier said than done, so here's another exercise to help you master it. It's particularly helpful when you have a situation where you are likely to feel uncomfortable. An athlete we work with uses this exercise when he's about halfway into a timed rowing piece when his legs are feeling heavy, his heart rate is beginning to rise and his mind is telling him he could simply stop and get off the rowing machine.

Saying yes or no[12]

Right now, take a break from reading this book and start by looking around.

As your eyes land on something, notice what it feels like to look at it from the point of view of 'no' – where 'no' means 'that's not good, I don't want it, that has to change, that's unacceptable'. Scan the room and for each thing you see adopt a 'no' approach to it over and over again. For example, you see a mug and say 'I don't want you', or your favourite book and say 'That has to change', or maybe your cat jumps on your lap for a cuddle and you say 'That's unacceptable'. Do this for everything you see for 30 seconds by saying it out loud.

Then add your body in. Put your body in a closed position – arms in, head down, eyes lowered, fists clenched, stomach muscles tightened. And from this position look around the room again and see each item from the point of view of 'no' for another 30 seconds. For example, you see your pen, and with arms crossed, head down, fists clenched say to it 'That's no good' and so on for everything you see.

Now repeat the exercise, only this time do it from the perspective of 'yes' – where 'yes' means 'that's ok, it doesn't have to change, I can allow it to be just as it is'. Look around the room again and for each specific thing you see adopt a 'yes' approach to it by saying yes out loud. Do this for 30 seconds. For example, you spot your smelly socks on the floor and say 'That's Ok' or your best T-shirt and say 'I can allow it to be just as it is' and so on.

Then add your body in again, only this time with an open posture – sitting or standing upright, arms out, eyes forward, head up, feet apart. You may want to think about your tone of voice as well, using a more soft and positive one than a harsh no. Now see the items in the room from this 'yes' mindset for 30 seconds. For example, a crack in the wall, saying 'Yes that's ok, I like it being there' or a wonky picture frame 'Yes you are fine just as you are'.

Take a deep breath and recall how different the world seems inside 'yes' versus 'no'. What's different?

You can try this exercise with a part of your training that you find uncomfortable. For example, a fitness test or a tactical move you find hard. Go through the exercise again, this time instead of noticing what you see, notice what you feel. For example, you might feel your legs burning or the urge to stop. Notice how different it is from a 'yes' as opposed to a 'no' mindset.

Next time you face a pressure situation where your nerves crank up, notice if your body or mindset is taking a 'no' stance. If they are, you can purposefully choose to shift your body and mindset into a much more open posture and an *Accept Being Uncomfortable* mindset of 'yes' – just like wearing your wrinkled socks – so you can focus on what's important to do. That way, you can explore your potential as an athlete.

What's in your kitbag?

Added to your kitbag, in this chapter is the knowledge we all face uncomfortable thoughts and feelings when the pressure is on in sport and in life. That's because, when you play sport, you are doing something that matters to you. Feeling pressure is not a sign of weakness, nor a fixed response determined by your DNA, and you don't have to always 'feel great' to perform well.

What's vital is how you respond to this pressure. As you *Drop the Struggle,* instead of fighting the anxiety or lack of confidence, you can keep the struggle switch in the off position. Accepting or saying yes to your thoughts and feelings, like wearing a wrinkled sock, enables you to *Play in the Now* and use your energy to perform at your best.

When you *Accept Being Uncomfortable* by saying 'yes' to the feelings, you can find and stay in the stretch zone more often, so that you know what you are truly capable of.

In Chapter 5, we'll introduce you to the last skill in your kitbag – *Do What Matters*. This chapter is about making sure there is purpose and meaning in the sport you do and the activities that sustain it. Whether you run, jump, swim, ride or shoot, whatever your sport, you need a roadmap to perform at your best.

Chapter **5**

Do what matters

---

*'Would you tell me, please, which way I ought to go from here?' 'That
depends a good deal on where you want to get to,' said the Cat.*
LEWIS CARROLL, ALICE IN WONDERLAND

It would be great if there was a simple formula for success in sport.
Whether your aim is to win an Olympic medal, to travel to a world cup
final or be selected for your local team, we'd each love some form of
checklist to follow to achieve these sporting dreams.

Unfortunately, there is no simple checklist. There is no easy ride.
There is no guarantee of success. It's partly what makes sport so rewarding, but also so challenging.

The journey ahead

We'd like you to think of your sporting dreams like a journey. When you
want to get somewhere, whether you take a train or plane, you drive
or you walk, you cycle or you run, you couldn't set off unless you knew
three key things:

- **The destination** – where are you going?
  Without a destination, you'd either wander aimlessly from
  place to place, feeling frustrated each day that you'd never

really arrived anywhere; or you'd simply stay at home and never even set off on your journey. The world would stay small and undiscovered.

- **The purpose** – why are you going there?
  When you lack purpose and don't know why you are going on a journey, it's easy to forget to take essential supplies, or the right equipment, some fuel and spares to get you there, making the journey uncomfortable. And when you don't have a clear handle on what's important to you, you might end up going to one place, when your passion and energy actually lie somewhere else.

- **The directions** – how do you get there?
  Without directions, you'd waste so much time going down blind alleys, taking wrong turns that at worst you'd just get lost and never get to your destination. At best it would certainly be dark before you got to the end of your journey.

The same is true for your sporting journey. When you don't have a destination, a purpose and some directions, you can put lots of effort into training, but struggle to improve, under-perform, or just be dissatisfied with the outcome of your achievements.

The destination – where am I going?

It's very common in sport psychology (and at school or in business) to think about the destination you want to get to. For example, your destination might be:

- to go to the Olympic Games
- to win a championships
- to be selected for a team
- to achieve a particular score or time in competition

In sport psychology we call these destinations 'goals'. We ask the question 'what do you want to achieve this year, this season, this month?' The list is endless. Goals are where we want to get to in our sport. Like places on our travel bucket list, goals can be crossed off that list. Goals can be completed and achieved.

Let's use an example here to illustrate. As a child, Shereena dreamt of going to the Olympics. She remembered watching the Games when she was only eight, inspired by the amazing feats in swimming, gymnastics and athletics. Etched in her brain were the 200-m sprint winning times. They felt like an impossible aspiration but one she secretly hoped for. In her early teens, she found out she was quite a good sprinter. In the back of her head, all the training sessions and countless competitions were a stepping stone to being good enough to represent her country at the Olympics one day.

Dream outcome

What is your dream outcome … your biggest goal or aspiration? Don't put limits on yourself here, think big!

Write this down in a notebook.

The good news is you've just put out into the universe your biggest, most audacious goal. And writing a goal down or even better sharing it with someone else increases our chance of achieving that goal.

But here's the rub. We can't guarantee we'll achieve our goals, especially our dream outcome.

Shereena's dream outcome was to compete at the Olympics. Unfortunately, despite being a fast runner and training five days a week from her teens to her mid-20s, she never achieved this goal. At each race she looked around at her peers and felt they were taller and better than her; surely they would find out soon that she wasn't that good. Increasingly, training became a chore and competing was just another opportunity to fail. Eventually, she stopped running altogether, feeling dissatisfied and unfulfilled.

Like Shereena, most of us spend too much of our energy focussed on the destination – the goal. Whilst it is helpful to have a dream outcome to aim at, we usually find that goals are not what matters most. We'd like to challenge you to think differently about your sporting journey.

The purpose – why am I going on a journey?

Whilst it might not seem obvious, knowing *why* we want to go somewhere or achieve something can have an even more powerful impact on our performance. Why we are competing in our sport and what's important to us together provide a solid foundation for high levels of performance and satisfaction. Our 'why' gives us the reason why something matters beyond ourselves. Whilst a goal requires an achievable action that can be ticked off, doing what's important to us demands an ongoing behaviour – how to act on an ongoing basis; how you want to treat yourself, others and the world around you.

And helpfully, there is a tool we can use to guide us. Our values. Values act like a compass to help us to set off on – and stay on – the path towards performing well and getting the most from sport and life. We use them to choose the direction we want to move in and to help keep us on track as we go. Values are lived, not achieved. When you act on a value, it's like heading east, no matter how far east you travel, there's always further to go. Whereas goals are the things you try to achieve on your journey, such as the mountain you want to climb, the medal you want to win or the beach you want to surf.

Our values motivate us to put in our best performance. Values also point us to what's important in our sporting life, and in all the other parts of life too. For example, challenge might be one of your values, and this might mean you take on more and more testing gym routines despite feeling completely out of your comfort zone. On the other hand, you might value fun, and so you'd thrive in and enjoy a training environment where you could factor in some things that were lighthearted and made you and the squad laugh.

Let's go back to Shereena. One of her values was excitement. Instead of focussing entirely on the success or failure of qualifying for the Olympics, it may have been better to spend time living her value of excitement as she trained and competed. For Shereena, having a value of excitement meant seeking, creating and enjoying activities that were stimulating and thrilling. Travelling to far-flung places, meeting new people, trying the latest kit, pushing the boundaries of her performance, she could enjoy these elements regardless of whether she qualified for the Olympics.

> Understanding our 'why' can have a huge impact on sporting outcomes. A great example of this is the British Women's hockey team who won the Rio 2016 Olympic final against the favourites, Netherlands. The team had invested time, effort and energy over many years in building a purpose-driven culture which aimed to 'Create history and inspire a generation'.[1] Their focus was about looking to the future and considering the positive impact they could have on sport, women's sport and society more broadly. They put a daily focus on what was important for each person and the squad as a whole. That 'why' inspired their gold medal performance.

We believe that our values should determine the direction we go in as we do our sport. Values are the foundation for doing our sport and performing well. Our values show us how we want to act or behave on an ongoing basis. They are the starting point that shapes the choices and decisions we make about our goals and dreams. And whatever our sport, when our training and competition are driven by values, the outcome is that we feel more energised, purposeful and engaged in what we are doing.[2]

Ivan Lendl coached previous world number one tennis player Andy Murray to his first two grand slam titles and his gold medal at the 2012 London Olympics. Lendl understood the importance of values and is famously said to have helped his protege to appreciate that having fun as he trained and competed helped to sustain his performance.[3]

Here are some simple truths about values:

- Values are **different for everybody**, and they can **change over time**. For example, at the start of your sports career, adventure might be a really important value for you. So you might want to choose a sport or set goals which mean you'll travel to different places. But if you've spent the last five years competing in different countries, you might find yourself missing your family, and so the value of relationships might become more important in this phase of your life.

- Values are **freely chosen**. They are things you choose for your life to be about. They should not be chosen by someone else, or based on other people's responses. Just because your friends or family value persistence, doesn't mean that you need to make persistence an important value for you. You get to decide what's important to you and what your values are.

- Values are **a direction** – not a destination or goal. This is a really important one to understand. We will never fully complete or achieve our values, they are not goals to tick off in our life. For example, getting into the GB Team is a goal, but being a good team-mate is a value. Our values will always be present to provide meaning and guide our actions.

- And lastly, values are **universal**. We can use them as a compass in all aspects of our life, not just in our sport. We can live our values in many different situations and ways, informing how we choose to act in all the different parts of our lives.

There are also some really important things to note about what values are NOT.

- Values are **not just about being happy**. Living to our values is usually fulfilling and meaningful, but not always about feeling happy. Following them can mean you have to do difficult and uncomfortable things. For example, as a coach who values honesty, you have to make tough selection decisions to pursue the best chance of success. Or as an athlete who values commitment you have to suffer through painful training sessions to make the marginal gains required.

- Values are also **not about being right or wrong**. Everyone has their own values. They will be different, between team-mates, colleagues, friends, families and even partners.

- Values are **not rules to live by**. You can hold your values lightly, and yet you should pursue them vigorously as you train and compete. Holding them lightly recognises that values are not rules or commandments to live by; they are flexible guides to help us go in the direction of what is important.

- Values are also **not how people treat us**. Sometimes people state values along the lines of a desire for how they would like to be treated – for example to be loved, or to be included or respected. These are things controlled by others, whereas values are about how individuals want to behave and what they want to stand for.

- Finally, **values are not feelings**. Feelings vary from moment to moment and are an internal state. Values are actions or qualities of action and endure over time.

Finding your Values Compass

There are different ways to identify the values that are important to you.

One way to get in touch with your values is to imagine your life at some point in the future. Have a go at this exercise.

Exercise – Retirement party

Imagine that you have reached the end of your sporting career, and you have decided to retire. There is a celebration in your honour and all of your team-mates, coaches, supporters and significant people are there. (Imagine this any way you like).

Some people imagine vivid pictures, as on a TV screen. Others imagine more with words or sounds or abstract ideas. However, you imagine it is right for you.

Also, remember this is your imagination – so it doesn't have to obey the rules of logic. It's okay if your parents or friends are there and they look exactly the same as they do today.

Stay alert for the million and one sneaky way your mind can try to pull you out of this exercise. Any time your mind starts interfering, making provocative comments; simply say 'Thank you mind!' and come back to the exercise.

So, imagine your retirement party – and everybody you care about is there to honour you.

Of all the people there, pick out three people who mean a lot to you and who have had a significant impact on you and your sporting career.

Imagine each of these people gets up to make a short speech about you – they may briefly talk about your sporting achievements, but most of all they talk about the person you are, the life you've lived, the way you conducted yourself and interacted with others, what you stood for and what you meant to them. Imagine that they say and mean whatever it is you would most like to hear them say and mean.

Notice how you feel as they say these things.

Take a moment to reflect on what you've heard. Jot these things in your notebook. And consider what does this tell you about what really matters to you, deep in your heart?

A second way to get in touch with your values is to think about your sporting heroes. Try this exercise.

Exercise – Heroes[4]

Think about people you admire in sport.

These could be people who have played a direct role in your life – family members, friends, teachers, coaches, team-mates, or it could be famous players, coaches and sporting legends who have inspired you.

Who would you most like to be like? Pick two to three people you really admire.

Now think about all the qualities that you really admire in these people – not that they won a medal, or scored a record number of runs or other sporting feats, but the personal qualities you see in them. Perhaps they were determined, selfless, creative

or a great team player. Or they were an inspiring leader or someone who always gave 100%.

Write these down.

Look back at the last two exercises now. What qualities came up? You
might have written down things like 'resilient', 'thoughtful', 'creative',
'ambitious' and so on. Think how you are like or unlike these qualities.
Refine the list down to five qualities that you would like to be known
for in your sport (and your life more generally). These form your Values
Compass.

My Values Compass

In your notebook, copy down the Values Compass and add these
five values to it.

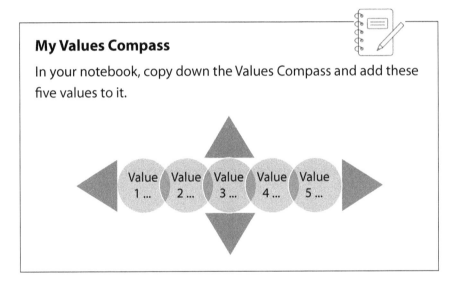

Your Values Compass reminds you how you want to behave in training
and competition. They prompt you every step of the way as you pursue
your goals; how you want to behave if and when you achieve your
goals; and how you want to behave if and when you fail to achieve
your goals.

Your values shape how you want to behave, whether in training or competition. One of Alison's sporting heroes is David Hemery, who in 1968 smashed the world record to win the men's 400-m hurdles at the Mexico City Olympics. From lane six, he had the courage to stick with his race plan and overhaul the favourites for the event. Coming into the event with the sixth fastest personal best, he won by over eight metres, causing the BBC commentator at the time to say 'Hemery won that from start to finish'.[5] After watching that race and reading accounts of it, one of the qualities she admires in Hemery is courage. In her work with athletes and coaches, it is one of the qualities that she would like to be known for too.

We'd like you to press the pause button here. If you rushed through the last section and don't have the five qualities that make up your Values Compass, go back and take some time to complete the Retirement Party or Heroes exercises earlier in this chapter.

We'll use your Values Compass to build your sport roadmap.

How do I get there? My sport roadmap

You've spent some time thinking about where you want to get to in your sport – your destination. And you have your Values Compass to help you navigate the journey from where you are right now (your purpose). Let's use this insight to plan the roadmap for your journey (your directions). This roadmap might be different from one you've done before as we'll use your values to help set the direction. You'll need a notebook for this section.

A canoeist we recently worked with, Benjie, was in the top twenty in the world. His dream outcome was being world number one. Working with his coach to set goals to help him to achieve this dream, he found himself struggling with his strength – it just wasn't where it needed to be. That left him slightly off the pace when it came to competitions, and he missed out on medals because of it.

His sport roadmap was based on a very rigid and regimented approach to strength and working in the gym. It was only when he created his Values Compass and realised that fun was a crucial part of what motivated him to train each day that his strength started to improve. He made sure that fun was baked into all his gym goals, and his approach to competition. Once he'd done that, he leapt five places up the world rankings.

My sport roadmap

Step 1: Chose a valued direction

There are many ways to get to your dream outcome. Few are straight. Often our path takes many twists and turns, with set-backs along the way. That's why we need our Values Compass.

To start with, pick one of the qualities or values you identified in your Values Compass that you'd really like to live by. It might be adventure, encouragement, skilfulness, excitement, self-development or respect, for example.

(You can repeat this process with each of the values from your Values Compass)

Step 2: Set your goals

Write down a graduated series of goals, starting from tiny simple goals that can be achieved right away to long-term goals that may not be achieved for months or years that are in service of the value that you've chosen.

For example, if you're a rower and encouragement is a key value for you, you might want to focus on giving positive feed-back to your team-mates during training, whether you are in the top boat or not. Or as a rugby player, if skilfulness is important to you, you might set yourself a goal of becoming the club's best kicker within the next five to ten years.

Create a list or table such as this one.

An Immediate Goal (something small, simple, easy, I can do in the next 24 hours that will lead me towards living my chosen value)

Short-Term Goal(s) (things I can do over the next few weeks that will lead me towards living my chosen value)

Medium-Term Goal(s) (things I can do over the next few months that will lead me towards living my chosen value)

Long-Term Goal(s) (things I can do over the next few years that will lead me towards living my chosen value)

This section may take you a few attempts. Take your time. Here are some tips to help make sure you're setting these goals as effectively as possible.

- Focus your goals on actions you can do rather than thoughts and feelings that you want to have or avoid.
- Make sure these actions are in your control (and not actions that you want other people to take).
- Make the goals specific enough so that you'll know when you've achieved them. This might include setting a time frame within which to complete them.
- Goals that stretch and challenge you are the most effective type of goals. But this may come with discomfort as you take

steps to achieve them, or uncertainty about whether you will achieve them. Acknowledge these feelings and check in with yourself that you are prepared to keep going when things are difficult. If the goals you have set don't feel somewhat uncomfortable or uncertain, perhaps they are not challenging enough.

- As you set your goals, keep checking back in with two things: (1) Your dream outcome – make sure that the goals you set will lead you towards that outcome and (2) Your values – make sure your goals are aligned with what is most important to you.

Step 3: Identify the benefits

Writing down your goal is a great step, but that's not all that's required. Let's take a few moments to clarify for yourself what the most positive outcome or outcomes of achieving your goals would be.

What would achieving this goal give you? How would it help you to become the person or performer you want to be? What impact might it have on others, or the world?

Make a note of the benefits of achieving your goals.

For example, let's go back to our example of the rower who valued encouragement. Achieving a goal of giving positive feedback to his team-mates every training session may benefit the squad as a whole by setting a positive, motivational climate across the whole team. It may help to create a team where encouragement is given freely and frequently, and confidence is the highest it's ever been.

If you find yourself struggling for the motivation to follow your roadmap, it can be helpful to come back to these and remind yourself of the benefits.

Make a commitment

As we said earlier, to enhance your chance of succeeding with your roadmap, there is some evidence that if you make a public commitment to your goals (i.e. if you state your goals to at least one other person) then you are more likely to follow through.

You've already committed to this by writing your goals down. The next step is to tell someone else what your goals and commitments are. Doing this encourages you to hold yourself accountable for what you said you were going to do. If you're feeling brave enough, you could even post it on social media. Making a public declaration is another way of increasing commitment.

Here are a few other helpful tips for increasing commitment to your goals:

- Record your progress: keep a journal, graph or drawing that plots your progress.

- Make it visible: keep it somewhere that you can see it, so you are constantly reminded about what you are working towards. Maybe you could stick it on the fridge, or on the mirror where you brush your teeth.

- Reward yourself for making progress towards your goal. Every step in the right direction is progress, so you deserve to give yourself recognition for that. Small rewards help push you on to major success. (A reward might be as simple as saying to yourself, 'Well done! You made a start!')

Sometimes it is helpful to find simple practical ways to make a commitment to our goals. India is a bobsleigh athlete. She was strong and fast, but her general cardio fitness wasn't good enough for world-class performances. So she set herself the goal of running twice a week, every week for six months. She worked out this was a total of 52 runs. She bought herself a pinboard and 52 pins. She put the pins on the left-hand side of her board and drew a line down the middle with a picture of the world championships podium on the right. Every time she completed a run, she moved a pin to the right-hand side of her board, so she could visually see the progress she was making and keep herself honest with her goal.

What is holding you back?

You've done all the hard work in this chapter – thought about who you are as a person and what's important to you and linked that with a goal or goals you want to achieve.

But all this is easier said than done. It can be much easier to stay in your comfort zone than it is to tackle the big challenges that are necessary to succeed in your sport. You might have great intentions, but stuff gets in the way from that becoming reality. And that stuff can be a whole host of things – not getting selected, getting injured, losing motivation or becoming too anxious to really test yourself.

But it's key to remember that personal growth, meaningful change and ultimately achieving your goals mean stepping out of your comfort zone which inevitably brings up discomfort. To be willing to do the things that really matter to you, you also have to be willing to experience this discomfort.

Success comes with failure.
Elation comes with pain.
Happiness comes with sadness.
Celebration comes with distress.

Using the skills you are learning and will continue to learn in this book, the key is to be able to open up and make room for this discomfort.

You don't have to like it, but you must accept that it comes with the territory. Before you set out to face the challenges that matter to you, think ahead: What sort of discomfort is likely and are you willing to make room for it?

As well as internal struggles you have with yourself, there will likely be external difficulties. These can either throw you off track or serve as a powerful motivator to continue working towards what's important to you. Contemplating these challenges in advance will help you deal with them as and when they arise.

Complete these sentences:

If internal difficulties arise, thoughts and feelings such as:
_____, then I will remind myself of the following in order to make room for them: _____.
If external difficulties arise, such as: _____, then I will take the following steps to deal with them: _____.

What's in your kitbag?

Goal setting has been and always will be an important part of achieving success in sport. But there is more to *Doing What Matters* than simply figuring out what you want to achieve. In this chapter, you've picked up some key kitbag tools for your athletic journey that lead to your potential: a motivating direction, a strong Values Compass and a clear roadmap.

Identifying what is important to you deep down helps you to be the person and performer you want to be whilst going after your goals. Linking your goals to your values assists you to tap into your inner motivation when you need it most, to make decisions that you are proud of and ultimately to help you achieve more of what you want in sport and in life. These might not come to you straight away and may evolve over time, so take a curious and patient approach to this, and keep coming back to them on a daily, weekly or monthly basis to ensure they are fresh in your mind.

Of course, along the way to *Do What Matters*, events and situations will come along to throw you off track. Remember you also have skills in your kitbag to use your Observing Mind to be able to *Play in the Now*, *Drop the Struggle* and *Accept Being Uncomfortable* to help you to get back on track to achieving your dream and fulfilling your potential.

In Part II, we'll apply all this training to the common performance challenges of confidence, motivation and dealing with setbacks.

PART II

Applying the training

You have made great headway into learning and practising the basic skills needed to perform better. By using your Observing Mind to actively notice what's going on in your head, you no longer need to be pulled around by your mind. You won't be yanked off track and away from your dreams and aspirations.

So far, you know how to:

- *Drop the Struggle* by unhooking from unhelpful thoughts and feelings
- *Accept Being Uncomfortable* with the difficult thoughts and feelings that you experience under pressure, so they don't get in the way of doing the important things
- *Play in the Now* through being mindful, staying present and focusing on what's important
- *Do What Matters* and move forward by changing your behaviour, setting a direction and taking steps towards your dreams.

It would be lovely if your journey toward your sport ambitions was a smooth one; a gentle uninterrupted climb on the path up your mountain to achieve your dreams. However, we know from working with teams, coaches and individuals over many years, that along with the highs of sporting performance, come the lows. In our experience, the lows are nearly always tangled up with three specific challenges – a crisis of confidence, a dip in motivation and a knock after a setback or failure.

So let's now look at these three challenges of confidence, motivation and setbacks and apply everything that you've learned so far in this book. We'll show you how to use your Observing Mind and apply the skills to *Drop the Struggle, Accept Being Uncomfortable, Play in the Now* and *Do What Matters* to tackle these challenges. We'll build on what you know and add some new exercises to your kitbag of tools.

Remember that these four skills are dynamic. They work together and using one can help you with the others. For example, if you are struggling with your confidence and you decide to use one of the mindfulness tools to help you *Play in the Now*, it may also help you to take a step towards how you want to be as an athlete and take an action to *Do What Matters.* So, if you are facing one of these challenges, don't get too hung up on which of these skills you start with. Picking one and doing it is much better than worrying about which one to start with and so doing nothing.

It will take practice and may not be easy. After all, if you've never ridden a horse beforehand, you don't jump on a tall thoroughbred stallion for the first time and expect it to be easy or to master horsemanship on day one.

Let's go!

Chapter **6**

The confidence choice

We do not think ourselves into new ways of living, we live ourselves into new ways of thinking.[1]

RICHARD ROHR

At this point in the book, you might be patiently waiting for us to slip in a chapter teaching you about positive affirmations and how to use them to build your self-esteem. After all, isn't that what psychologists help you to do, show you how to keep saying positive things to yourself? Something like 'I am a great athlete', 'I am feeling strong today', 'I can still perform despite only getting five hours' sleep', 'We're the better team'. You can fill in your own version of positive self-talk here – you'll know what it is, we are sure.

And we imagine, if you are anything like us (and in fact most of the rest of the population), you can just as easily find negative things to say to yourself, such as 'I am a rubbish athlete', 'I am not feeling at all strong today', 'There's no way I can do well, I only got five hours sleep last night', or 'The other team has got some better athletes than us'.

The truth about confidence

We learnt in Chapter 3 that it's so easy to waste time, energy and effort on arguing back and forth with ourselves, trying to prove that we are confident and capable. Much as we try to fill our heads with positive affirmations, they just as easily slip away again. And sometimes, repeating positive self-statements to ourselves can even make us feel worse.[2]

Repeating positive self-statements does not always help us. Researchers found among participants with low self-esteem, those who repeated a positive self-statement ('I'm a lovable person') or who focussed on how that statement was true, felt worse than those who did not repeat the statement or who focussed on how it was both true and not true. Among participants with high self-esteem, those who repeated the statement or focussed on how it was true felt better than those who did not, but to a limited degree. The science shows us that repeating positive self-statements may benefit certain people, but backfire for the very people who 'need' them the most.[3]

The fact is we can't stop our mind from coming up with reasons why we are no good. Of course, we know our mind is only doing that to protect us, but however hard we work at stopping them, those pesky thoughts and uncomfortable feelings will keep showing up.

But the self-critical or destructive thoughts in themselves are not a problem, until they stop us from doing what's important to us.

Maybe you can relate to this story:

I'm about to step out onto the pitch. I'm feeling pretty nervous and having lots of thoughts like 'If I don't play well today, I won't get picked for the next game'. I look around me and everyone else seems to be totally in control. My team-mates are all smiling, talking to each other and have warmed up really well. Why do I feel so scared compared to them!? And when I look at the opposition, they seem totally on it, none of them seem nervous. I hope I don't get the ball to start with, I'll probably totally mess it up the state I'm in. I might just linger on the wing to avoid it for the first few minutes.

When we don't feel confident, it's easy to convince ourselves we are no good and talk ourselves out of doing the challenging things it takes to be good in our sport. We wait for the days when we are feeling really confident to be able to perform at our best.

The truth is, if we wait to feel confident before we are at our best, we might be waiting a very long time.

Imagine you are an athlete on the starting line of the 100 metres. Even if you were the best sprinter in the world, you can't know with 100% certainty that you will win the race.

Hopefully you will have banked the training you have done. You may have taken the right steps to fuel your body. It's likely you will have planned to get eight hours of sleep the previous night to enable your body to perform at its best. You can recall the last ten races that you have won. And you might have followed your coach's optimum training plan in the previous training cycle.

As a result of taking these actions, you may be feeling confident as you drop into the blocks on the starting line. But equally you may not. Doubt creeps in. Nerves too. There is no guarantee that you will feel confident as you step up to the start line.

But the great news (and a piece of news we hope will be a total game-changer for you) is **you don't have to feel confident to be able to perform at your best.**

Or phrased another way, you can still pull out a fantastic performance, even when you're nervous and doubting your own abilities.

This might be different from what you've heard before, so let's break it down a little. How can this be true? Previously you've been told that self-belief and confidence are vital ingredients for success. They can help, that's for sure. And on the days when you are feeling confident, make the most of it!

But, there is another way.

Do what matters: Confidence as an action

We limit ourselves as athletes if we think confidence is only about believing in ourselves and about our abilities to succeed at things. Instead, what if confidence was not a feeling, but an action?

What can we learn about the 'act' of trusting in ourselves and 'doing' confidence?

Go back to our example and imagine once again you are a sprinter lining up for the 100 metres. What if confidence was a simple act of trusting ourselves and of stepping confidently onto the starting line?

Psychotherapist, author and GP Dr Russ Harris backs the view that confidence starts with an action. He claims that: The action of confidence comes first, the feelings of confidence come later.[4]

To illustrate this, Harris recounts the story of Nelson Mandela's 27 years in prison. Mandela's biographer, Richard Stengel, captured how Mandela often felt afraid. Despite this, Mandela knew that to be a leader and inspire his colleagues, he had to step out and speak to the nation, even when he was scared. Although he could not control his feelings, he could control his facial expression and hold his body with confidence, so that those around him were inspired. According to Stengel, the sight of him walking proud and tall was enough to sustain the fellow prisoners for days.

Mandela was a great example of acting with confidence. He didn't wait until he felt confident or eliminated his fear before he stepped out as a leader, but he did take an act of trust. He trusted himself to walk tall. He learnt to rely on himself to take action, irrespective of how he was feeling. Confidence is an action.

An example from the sporting world is the great Usain Bolt. Having to defend his own Olympic title multiple times, there was no way that Bolt didn't feel a few nerves. But we never saw them, because he knew what he needed to do to 'be' confident first. His style was jovial, playful and light-hearted. He joked with the volunteers at the Olympic stadium and demonstrated big, bold gestures to the millions watching around the world. However he was feeling on that day, he went out there and acted confidently.

Confidence looks different to different people. Former world number one tennis player Roger Federer for example is not a flashy, jovial performer like Bolt. His style of confidence is focussed and determined. His actions are calm and smooth, his facial expressions consistent and his body language serene. In his own way, he knows what he needs to do when he steps on the court to 'be' confident in himself, regardless of how he is feeling inside.

> You're not always going to feel confident, that we know for sure. But by knowing how to go out there and 'be' confident, you can perform at your best regardless of how you're feeling. Oftentimes, 'being' confident will lead to you 'feeling' more confident. But if it doesn't, well, it doesn't actually matter. Because it's your actions and responses to what's going on that's the most important thing – and actually the only thing you can control.

You may be reading this thinking, 'Ah, this sounds like the motto "fake it till you make it"'. We don't think this is about faking it at all. This is about knowing what you're like at your best and being able to step out and embody that regardless of how you are feeling. It's about understanding yourself, noticing your own internal state and also knowing what you need to do to bring your top performance. It's still you, you're not trying to be anything else, only the best version of you.

Take a few moments now to consider how you can step out confidently, regardless of how you are feeling inside.

If I had unlimited confidence ...

Pick up your notebook. Set yourself a timer for five minutes. Then read the following questions and have a go at answering them.

> If you had unlimited confidence when you were playing your sport:
>
> How would you perform and compete differently?
>
> How would you behave differently towards others?
>
> How would you talk to yourself differently?
>
> How would your body language be different?

These things you have just written down are pretty sacred. These are things you can go out there and do, no matter how you are feeling. Wake up with a sense that you are a bit 'off'? That's ok – you have tangible things you can go and do anyway. And remember, don't try and ignore or push away what you're feeling … acknowledge it, accept it and go out there and be your best self.

Next time you have the opportunity to practise this, look at your list before you step out to perform. Perhaps pick one or two to focus on the first time around, and as you get more comfortable with acting confidently you can add in other layers.

Drop the struggle: It's normal to doubt yourself

We've learnt that confidence is an action, not just a feeling. The 'confidence as an action' strategy could well change your whole relationship with yourself and your performance.

But there will still be self-doubt. There will still be nerves.

We'll deal with the nerves in a moment. Let's first look at those doubts. Research tells us that there are some common confidence blockers, that is, thoughts that get in the way of our confidence. The three main ones are:

1. I don't believe I am good enough
2. I am never satisfied with my performance
3. I believe that something will go wrong

Perhaps you can relate to one or all of these. Or perhaps you have other confidence-blocking thoughts that try to get in the way.

This is where defusion – or dropping the struggle – comes in again.

Practising the *Drop the Struggle* strategies you have learnt so far in this book (in Chapter 3) will help you continue to separate from your thoughts, realise they are just thoughts and they aren't necessarily true.

Here's another fun strategy to try. Find a quiet moment and spend two minutes on this simple exercise to stretch yourself and develop a new way of thinking.

Musical thoughts[5]

Bring to mind a negative self-judgement or critical thought that commonly bothers you and gets in the way of you feeling your confident best. For example, 'I'll never be as good as him' or 'I always crumble under pressure'.

Hold that thought in your mind and really believe it as much as you can for about ten seconds. Notice how it affects you.

Now take that same thought and sing it to yourself to the tune of 'Happy Birthday'.

Sing it silently inside your head. Notice what happens.

Now go back to the thought in its original form. Once again, hold it in your mind and believe it as much as you can, for about ten seconds. Notice how it affects you.

Now take that thought and sing it to the tune of 'Jingle Bells'. Sing it silently inside your head. Notice what happens.

The aim of this activity is to encourage you not to take your thoughts quite so seriously – after all, they are just thoughts! After doing this exercise, you probably found that you're holding that thought a little more lightly and you're not buying into it quite as much. Perhaps a weight has been lifted and you're more able to focus on actions and behaviours rather than letting your thoughts dominate you.

Even the most successful athletes need to learn how to *Drop the Struggle* with their thoughts and feelings. Michael Phelps is the most decorated Olympian of all time, with 23 gold, three silver and two bronze medals in his sport of swimming. Since retiring, people have been surprised to learn he grappled with anxiety and a lack of confidence throughout his career. He is quoted as saying 'As an athlete, it's challenging, especially for a male. We're supposed to be big and strong and macho, not somebody who struggles with their emotions. But we're all human beings'.[6,7] It seems that reaching the top in sport doesn't stop us from grappling with difficult thoughts and feelings.

One of the key messages of this chapter is that self-doubt is normal, critical and judgemental thoughts are normal, and a lack of confidence at times when you need it most – is normal. Remember our brains are wired to think critically and judgementally, so it makes sense that we are critical of ourselves. Trying to pretend we are fine, ignoring those thoughts or pushing them away, only makes things worse.

We suggest that you try something different. Rather than attempting *not* to think something, try holding those thoughts more lightly, putting things in perspective and realising that they are just thoughts and they don't have to have a hold over you. Musical thoughts are a great way of doing this. It might take you a while to get into it and *Drop the Struggle* with the thoughts. But like anything, the more you do it the quicker and easier it will become.

If you're still wondering why we aren't focussing on teaching you to think positive thoughts to build your confidence, this metaphor might help you.

Picture this – you are taking some time to chill out and are sitting down quietly to read one of your favourite books. Then, the next-door neighbours' builders arrive and start drilling right outside your window. You want to ignore it, but the more you try to push the sound out, the more it seems to annoy you. You get out your headphones and put on a playlist instead, hoping to drown out the noise. But it's no good, the noise is annoying you now, and it won't go away. As a result, your nice relaxing down time has been ruined.

In some ways, this is a bit like how our minds work. We can be going about our lives, playing our sports or engaging in other activities we enjoy, when a negative voice starts chattering in our minds. It's not helpful, neither is it pleasant to listen to, but we can't just switch it off. So, what do we do? Well sometimes we try to drown out this negative voice by using positive thinking. 'If I can think positively, the annoying negative thoughts will go away' we might believe. But positive thinking is a bit like bringing in a second noise trying to drown out the first. Doing this makes it very hard to focus your attention on what you're trying to do because your mind is busy with two noises playing in the background.

Rather than blocking the noise out, dropping the struggle means just noticing it, accepting it and letting the struggle go. You're not focussing your energy and attention on trying to push it away or get rid of it, and therefore you're not placing any importance on what it's got to say. It can be helpful to name it when you notice it playing – 'ah here's the racket playing in my head' or 'oh there's my mind worrying or predicting the worst' or 'there's the I'm going to mess up story'.

Whatever noise is going on for you, just notice it without judgement and name it so you don't get into a battle with these thoughts. Just let them come and go like a noise playing in the background and instead focus your attention and your energy on doing what's important to you – taking action confidently.

Play in the now: Pay attention

We know by now that the actions of confidence can come before the feelings of confidence. If our Thinking Mind is time-travelling, taking our thoughts off in all kinds of directions – replaying the past or fretting about the future – it's hard for us to run well, jump really high, catch a flying ball and so on. Performing well helps our confidence and that requires us to engage fully in what we are doing.

It's hard to stay confident and play well when our mind is not focussed in the present. During Wimbledon in 2022, Australian maverick tennis player Nick Kyrgios got distracted by a member of the crowd shouting at him. He complained to the umpire, getting more and more angry that nothing was being done about it. After that incident, he wasn't able to focus back in on the match or play his game well. His performance went downhill from there, and he went on to lose the match.[8]

Kyrgios's experience shows just how vital it is to stay present in the here and now, and not let your mind pull you around with thoughts from the past that you can't do anything about. Being lost in our thoughts or going through the motions on autopilot is unlikely to deliver our best performance. We need to engage fully in doing our sport.

You already know how to engage in what you are doing. You know how to pay attention. The mindfulness practices that you've learnt so far (in Chapter 2) and practised on a regular basis can reap great benefits for your overall confidence each day.[9] Learning to *Play in the Now* isn't just for big performances.

Here's another short activity which you can practise to develop your ability to bring your focus and attention back to the present moment.

The mindful finger

Sit down with your feet squarely on the floor. Put your forefinger on your thigh, half way between your knee and your hip.

Hold it there and just pay attention to your breath for a few moments.

Then draw attention to your thoughts, and notice where they go.

If you start thinking about something in the past, pull your finger back towards you. If you start thinking about something in the future, push your finger towards your knee. When you are just thinking about your breath, move it to the middle.

See how aware you are of your thoughts. It doesn't matter how much your finger moves, the key is to recognise when your mind wanders – which we know it will.

Practising this activity on a regular basis will help you to tap into and be more aware of your own thoughts. To recognise when they are dragging you away from playing in the now and taking action confidently. The more you practise this in the quiet moments, the better you'll be able to do it in situations when you most need to step forward with confidence.

Accept being uncomfortable: The stuck loop

Doing things with confidence isn't easy. So far, you've explored strategies to *Do What Matters* and take action, as well as *Drop the Struggle* and deal with the doubts that come along. You've also got strategies to *Play in the Now*, for when you are not fully engaged in the activity you are doing. But what if you are still not training confidently, competing confidently, leading the team confidently and so on?

Well, it's likely you are caught in a 'stuck loop'.[10]

Picture football player Vittorio. Vittorio has been playing really well out on the wing, coming home from games feeling happy and confident, playing is fun. He's skilled at taking a ball and passing it accurately. He really likes the buoyed up feelings he's experiencing. To develop his game, his coach wants to take him out of his comfort zone and spend some time at centre-forward. Naturally, Vittorio wants to hold onto his feelings of happiness and confidence, but after his first training session at centre-forward he's suddenly feeling embarrassed, foolish, discouraged and a little bit anxious. Surely everyone is judging him and thinking he's got two left feet? He doesn't know where to move or what his role is in this new position.

Vittorio isn't comfortable with all these new and difficult feelings of embarrassment, anxiety, isolation and so on. In fact he wants to avoid them at all costs. So to do this, he finds excuses why his passes go awry or can't aim a shot at goal. He misses training two weeks in a row so he doesn't have to feel foolish whilst he's learning the new position. He tells himself the reason why he can't get the hang of this new position is because he's not trying hard yet. He tries some positive affirmations, but doesn't believe any of them.

Avoiding playing or not trying makes Vittorio feel better – at least in the short term. Those feelings of embarrassment or foolishness have gone away for a bit. But he can't do that forever. He wants to play football. Deep down he also wants to improve his game and knows how important it is to get a wider experience of positions and skills. But as soon as he goes back to training as centre-forward, those feelings come flooding back and his confidence drains.

He's in a 'stuck loop'.

To break out of his stuck loop, Vittorio can do the three steps in the exercise below to *Accept Being Uncomfortable.* Take three minutes to try this for yourself right now.

The soft flexible container[11]

1. Go back to the answers you wrote down earlier in the chapter for the exercise 'If I had unlimited confidence when I was playing my sport I would ….'. Choose one of them that you'd like to do.
2. Sit quietly and ask yourself, what feelings am I willing to experience, so that I can act confidently and do this action?

For example, am I willing to feel rejected / helpless/ confused / discouraged / foolish / weak / stupid / ashamed and so on.

3. Think about the action you've chosen. Are you uncomfortable just thinking about it? Notice the discomfort in your body.

4. Name these feelings such as 'I am noticing I am feeling tense' or 'I am noticing I am feeling weak'.

5. Then make room for these feelings by imagining yourself as a soft flexible container for them. Instead of trying to get rid of the feelings you have named or squash them or not think about them, make room for them in your expandable container. However big the feeling is that you feel, your container flexes to that size.

6. Finally, imagine carrying these feelings with you as you do the action you've chosen.

We step out of our stuck loop when we are prepared to make space for the emotional highs, along with the uncomfortable lows, that both come with playing sport. Being willing to make space in your container for all your feelings, without judging or suppressing them, allows you to act confidently, whatever your sport.

What's in your kitbag?

You've put another big idea into your kitbag in this chapter.

You could wait your whole career to *feel* confident or not have any doubts before you go for your goals and dreams. There will have been many times you haven't felt confident in the past, and there will be many times that you won't feel confident in the future. If you wait for that confident feeling or try to remove all your doubts every time you compete, you'd waste opportunities, have lots of 'if only's' and never know how good you could be in your chosen sport. You don't have to be certain you'll be successful, you just have to acknowledge that you could be. Fears, doubts and lack of confidence can constrain you, but you don't know what you're capable of unless you decide to explore what is unknown, what's possible.

This chapter has shown you that confidence is not just a feeling – it's also something you do. Whatever the situation, you can pull a range of exercises out of your kitbag:

- Employing your Observing Mind and playing musical thoughts to help you *Drop the Struggle* with them

- Using the soft flexible container to *Accept Being Uncomfortable* with the feelings of not being confident

- Mindfully recognising your thoughts by putting a finger on your leg to pay attention to what's important as you *Play in the Now*

Together, these allow you to go and *Do What Matters*, that is, all the things you'd do if you had unlimited confidence!

Let's take a look at the next challenge – motivation – in Chapter 7.

Chapter 7

Create the energy to succeed

When a great ship is in harbor and moored, it is safe, there can be no doubt. But that is not what great ships are built for.
CLARISSA PINKOLA ESTES

Motivation is fundamental to succeeding as an athlete.

Sometimes we are able to tap into our energy resources easily as we feel connected to our values and deeper intrinsic motivation. We do the things that are important to us. Other times, we experience dips or slumps in energy and motivation. We avoid situations, procrastinate or opt out of things we know deep down will take us in the direction we want to go.

Like our discussion of confidence in Chapter 6, motivation is also an action – regardless of what thoughts and feelings are going on for you, motivation is about acting in line with your values and doing things that take you in the direction you want to go.

We sometimes think that successful athletes are motivated all of the time. The COVID-19 pandemic provided a very real challenge to motivation for many athletes. A research team from institutions all across the globe surveyed 12,256 athletes from 142 countries. The study revealed that elite-level athletes suffered low motivation during the movement restrictions (e.g. lockdowns) associated with the COVID-19 pandemic.[1] Although this was an exceptional event, it shows how normal it is for our motivation to take a knock, particularly when events seem out of our control.

Using the Values Compass for motivation

Our values influence our attitudes and behaviours, our drives and motivations and affect the decisions we make as we go through life.

As we've learnt, we all have different values and things that drive us. For example, some are driven by success, others by a desire to learn and others by family, fun or freedom. Most of us have many values. However, there are some values that are more dominant than others.

In Chapter 5 you created a Values Compass of your special core values, to keep you moving towards your goals in sport. We'll revisit these core values in this chapter, to uncover how they affect your motivation to train, compete, perform and live your life.

How do our values motivate us?

Take, for example, Karly, a professional squash player. Her driving force is to win a major tournament, underpinned by a Values Compass of achievement, challenge, trust, honesty and courage. Motivated by this, she can put herself through a demanding fitness regime and travel the world, even if that means sacrificing relationships, because she values achievement, courage and being challenged.

Or another example – Jamal is a handball player who values health, fun and pushing himself to the limit. Jamal injured his wrist and had to take some time away from the sport. This meant that he couldn't live by his values in the way he normally would. His mental and physical health was affected because he couldn't train; he wasn't having fun because he couldn't play his sport, and there was no way he could push himself to the limit with the injury he had. Not being able to live by his values hugely impacted Jamal's life during that period. Had he been more aware of his Values Compass, he may have been able to find other ways to connect to his values away from the handball court as part of his rehabilitation.

Knowing what your values are and being able to connect with them on a day-to-day basis has a huge impact on your motivation. Even if you can't live your life in the way you normally would, there are ways of connecting with your values to still feel motivated each day.

In his retirement speech in August 2022[2] F1 driver Sabastian Vettel demonstrated the connection between his values and his motivation. Vettel said 'I love this sport, it's been central to my life for as long as I can remember ... Next to racing, I have grown a family and I love being around them ...My passion for racing and Formula One comes with lots of time spent away from them and takes a lot of energy. Committing to my passion the way I did and the way I think is right, no longer goes side by side with my wish to be a great father and husband ... My goals have shifted from winning races and fighting for championships, to seeing my children grow, passing on my values, helping them up when they fall, listening to them when they need me, not having to say goodbye and most importantly being able to learn from them and let them inspire me'.

This is a great example of how values drive motivation. The important things in Sebastian's life are personal growth, connection to others and learning. In the early years as a Formula One racing driver, these values motivated him to compete, win races and strive for success. Now later on in his life, he uses these values to drive himself to be a great father and husband, to connect to his family rather than a racing team, and to watch his children grow rather than grow himself. He is still living closely by his values and using them to motivate him to be better, but it is now in other domains of his life.

This example doesn't mean that we should all just quit our sports and retire to spend more time with our families, far from it. This is an example of consistently living your life aligned to your values, and continually checking in that you are doing so, perhaps making adjustments where needed.

When you find yourself demotivated, disconnected from your values or just a bit lost, have a go at the following activity. It can also be hugely beneficial to do this exercise proactively, so you are more aware on a day-to-day basis how to tap into your inner motivation.

Connecting values and motivation[3]

For this exercise we're going to encourage you to do something a bit different, so you'll need some paper and pens handy.

1. Take a few moments to think back and recall an event, or a moment when you were playing your sport where you felt especially motivated. See if you can find an actual moment when you felt particularly driven to be your best self, when you felt in flow, or empowered to achieve something great.

Bring into your mind details of who else was there, what you were doing and feeling or thinking. What could you hear, see and smell? Relive that moment as fully as you can.

2. As you reflect on that special moment, consider which of your values (from your Values Compass in Chapter 5) you were demonstrating. How were you acting?

For example, maybe trust is in your Values Compass. You recall a time when you trusted yourself to commit to taking a penalty for your team. When you followed this value of trust, you felt excited in your body as you stepped forward to take the penalty, walking calmly to the spot and striking the ball firmly and decisively.

3.   Whilst thinking about that special moment or event, grab your paper and pens. Draw any picture that comes to mind that speaks to you about that value. There are no art prizes at play here. Allow your picture to form freely. You can doodle, sketch or scribble. Don't worry about the quality of the drawing, this is for your eyes only. The point is to consider, without words, what that great memory suggests about how and when you feel motivated.

4.   Once you have drawn it, take some time to reflect on your picture. What does the drawing tell you about your own motivation? What does this mean about what you stand for as an athlete? How do you act when you live this value? If there are a couple of words that capture this, write them under the picture.

5.   Keep this picture somewhere safe, or display it on your phone, desk or fridge so that when motivation dips, you can tap back into your most motivated self, and what you can do or be in this moment.

Connecting to your values and understanding how they drive your motivation help to steer you in the direction you want to head in your life and your sport. Once you are connected to these, you're in a much better place to work out what your actions should be.

Milkha Singh's[4] story reveals an athlete who saw how important values were in motivating him. Milkha was arguably India's best male track athlete, winning Commonwealth and Asian games gold medals. Caught in the partition of India and Pakistan, most of his family were killed in the troubles. As his father fell, his last words were 'Bhaag Milkha Bhaag', exhorting his son to run for his life.

The boy ran – first to save his life, and then to win medals. Arriving in India as an orphan in 1947, he discovered his athletic abilities in the army. Singh won Gold at the 1958 Commonwealth Games in Cardiff and went on to finish fourth in the 400 metres at the Rome Olympics, missing out on a bronze medal by a whisker. He was awarded the Helms World Trophy for winning an incredible 77 of his 80 international races.

Not long before he died in 2021, he talked about the link between his values and his motivation: 'We had nothing in our times. The athletes and sportsmen in those days didn't earn much money. We worked for the applause, people's appreciation inspired and motivated us, we ran for the country'. We can imagine that values such as adventure, gratitude and determination might have motivated this remarkable runner.

Do what matters: Focus on small actions

Setting yourself goals in life and sport is a great way to help motivate your day-to-day behaviour. In Chapter 5, you worked on your roadmap, considering your dream outcome, the valued direction you wanted to go in, and what might get in the way.

When you are struggling with motivation, one helpful strategy can be to keep your attention on immediate actions instead of endpoints. This will help you sustain a behaviour, especially when it's messy or difficult. We have a lot more control over our own behaviour than we do outcomes. For example, if you are trying to learn a new skill, if you only focus on results you're more likely to get discouraged when it's not going as well as you'd hoped or you make a mistake, or you may even stop doing it once you reach your goal.

Motivation comes in 'waves' and it's best to design small, easy behaviours that you'll keep doing even when your motivation is low.[5] Stretching whilst waiting for the kettle to boil will lead you more towards your goal of increased flexibility. Leaving your phone on the other side of your room means you have to get out of bed when your alarm goes off in the morning, meaning you're more likely to make it to training on time. These small, easy behaviours that take up limited energy and brain capacity can also be described as habits.

Habits are the small decisions you make and actions you perform every day. You get up and start your day with a coffee, you always take a sip of water before putting your gumshield in, you jump up and down twice before a race and so on. They are powerful because they are largely unconscious, thereby freeing up resources and energy for our brains to carry out other more complex tasks.

We all have habits, and we activate hundreds every day. Some we don't notice because they have been part of our lives for so long. Others help us to be the athlete we want to be, so we work hard at establishing and keeping them (like stretching after training, going to bed at the same time each night or meditating for ten minutes each day). Still others can take us away from being our best self (like procrastinating, spending hours on our phone or overtraining) and need to be changed.

Habits guide our daily behaviours and therefore determine the success of our goals. During times when we feel dips in motivation, setting ourselves up with healthy, helpful habits will help us to get back on track.

Before we explore how to set new habits, consider your current habits. Which ones help you to be the person and athlete you want to be? Which ones take you away from that?

Helpful and unhelpful habits

Step 1

Write down as many of your habits as you can think of. Bring to mind a typical day and consider all the things you do without really thinking about it.

Once you've done as many as you can, ask close friends or family members to add any they have noticed.

Step 2

Next, take those habits and, with a coloured pen or highlighter, mark the ones you think are helpful in one colour and one's you think are unhelpful in another colour.

For example, giving yourself ten minutes in the morning for yoga or stretching might be a helpful habit, because it helps you to be the athlete you want to be; going on your phone instead of completing your training diary in the evening might be an unhelpful one, as it takes you away from being the athlete you want to be.

Step 3

Being aware of behaviours you want to change is the starting point. Now take a look at your 'unhelpful' list. How aware are you of these on a daily basis? What's the potential impact they might be having on your motivation?

Now you've got a chance to change these.

A great way to start to develop healthier habits for directing your energy towards being the performer you want to be is the three Rs: Reminder, Routine and Reward.

First of all, reflect on one of your most unhelpful habits and decide on a habit that would be much more helpful for you to do instead. This may be something that's been on your mind for a while, or you may use the habit list you just created to prompt your thinking. Take some time to do this now, focussing on just one habit to start with.

Then, follow these three simple steps.

The three Rs of forming or changing a habit

1. Set yourself a **reminder** – put an alarm on your phone, print off and stick up a picture on the back of your door, or write it on a post-it note and leave it on your fridge. Any way that helps you to remember to engage in this habit.
2. Get into the **routine** – repeat the habit as often as you can. It's thought that habits take around 66 days to be fully ingrained (although some will take less time, and others more).[6] Get into the routine and stick to it, for as long as you can. It also needs to be realistic though, so make sure it's a schedule you can feasibly achieve and are motivated towards. If in doubt, start small and you can always increase it as time goes on.
3. Give yourself a **reward** – every now and then, allow yourself a reward for engaging in your habit. Make yourself your favourite breakfast after a morning gym session, or give yourself a random day off after you've learnt a new skill that you've spent one hour every morning practising.

Here's an example to help you see how this works, then it will be your turn to set your own habit. Let's use the example of training in the morning, or not as the case may be.

This might be your current habit:

Reminder – Your alarm goes off. This is the reminder that initiates a behaviour – to get out of bed. But you feel tired and so lean over and put the alarm on snooze. You repeat this four or five times, until you've missed the opportunity to train before work, it's too late now.

Routine – This happens so often, that it's become a routine. You know it's going to happen, so barely even fight it anymore.

Reward – You get extra time in bed. You get to curl up and enjoy the warmth of your bed for an extra half an hour. Bliss.

Except you know that this habit is not leading you towards the person and performer you want to be.

So let's change this habit around.

Reminder – The clock strikes 06.30 and your alarm goes off. The new alarm is loud and energetic, and what's more, you've left your phone on the other side of the room, so now you have to get up!

Routine – Every Monday, Wednesday and Friday, you set the same alarm leaving your phone in the same place across the other side of the room. These are the days you know you get straight out of bed.

Reward – It might be tough to begin with, but after a while you notice that you're feeling so much more alive in the mornings and throughout the day when you start your day with exercise. There is an intrinsic reward because you feel good in mind and body throughout the day, and don't have to be thinking about when you're going out running or to the gym. But extrinsic rewards never hurt either, so after a month of doing this, you treat yourself to something you love.

This is a super simple but highly effective way of setting positive, healthy habits to regain a sense of motivation and energy for your sport and training.

Helpful tips when starting your new habits:

Set up the environment

One of the biggest factors in whether we are successful in creating new habits is the physical environment around us. Not having junk food in the house makes you less likely to eat it. Putting your running clothes out the night before makes it more likely you'll go out running in the morning. And like our example, leaving your phone on the other side of the room means that you have to get up to turn it off. Try setting up the environment in advance to make life easy for yourself so you don't need the willpower to keep new habits.

Start small

The most common cause of unsuccessful change is biting off more than you can chew. The greatest example of this is New Year's resolutions when people seek to reinvent some part of their lives, but rarely follow through with it. Instead, when we start small, achieving the small goals gives us a hit of dopamine, leading to momentum. Small changes also accumulate over time. For example, to start the habit of finishing off your gym sessions with stretching, start with just two minutes of stretching and gradually build momentum to increase the chance of it becoming a long-lasting habit. Author James Clear[7] talks about the 20-second rule: if you can't start something within 20 seconds of a trigger, you are significantly less likely to do it.

Make a commitment

Make a commitment to yourself, to fully engage mentally in the new habit. This can be done through writing down and repeatedly reviewing your goals, or even better, letting other people know. By sharing habits you're trying to develop, you're taking advantage of one of the most powerful influences in the world: social pressure. Try putting up your progress in a place others can see it (e.g. the fridge), sharing it on social media or simply telling others about what you would like to achieve and requesting that they keep tabs on how you're doing.

Even with the best habits in the world, you will have some days where you wake up feeling exhausted, anxious and unmotivated for the day's activities, for no apparent reason. You will have self-sabotaging thoughts, convincing yourself that a rest day would be the best thing to do. Even if you have a goal you are really motivated to achieve, you will procrastinate over and over and put off doing the things you need to do to achieve it. After all, you are human!

Even though you are motivated to achieve your goal, sometimes you will get stuck in an endless spiral of avoiding the things that will get you there, such as training, skill practice, updating your log, speaking with the coach and so on. If you want to make the most of your potential in sport, you need to maximise your intrinsic motivation and deal with the self-destructive thoughts that might be trying to sabotage you. Using the kitbag of strategies you have learnt throughout this book will help you to do just that. Let's explore a few new ones to help you stay motivated.

Drop the struggle: Give your mind a name

In Chapter 1, we explored the concept of Thinking Mind and Observing Mind. One of the best ways to *Drop the Struggle* and create separation between yourself and your thoughts is to give your Thinking Mind a name. You may think we are barmy, but stay with us and you'll see the meaning behind what we're suggesting. If your Thinking Mind has a name, then it is different from 'you'. When you listen to someone else you can choose to agree with what they say or not, and if you don't want to cause conflict, it's best not to try to argue the person into agreement with you. That is the same with your internal voice. You can choose whether or not to listen to it and let it dictate what you do as an athlete.

Putting this into reality, let's take a scenario where you have a competition coming up, and your coach wants you to work on one specific aspect of your performance. For whatever reason, you're really not feeling motivated to do it, even though you know it will help. Everything in your Thinking Mind is telling you that it's not needed and you'll do just fine as you are. As soon as you have this thought, you're annoyed at yourself for being so lazy and cutting corners, so you try your best to muster up the motivation to do the practice your coach has suggested. You battle through, drag yourself along and all the while feel frustrated and tense in both your mind and body. The extra practice gets done but it's hard work and drains a lot of your mental and physical energy.

Alternatively, let's imagine as soon as that thought comes into your head, you recognise it as your mind (whom you've named Timmy) as being unhelpful. The same feelings are there, along with the thoughts of skipping the extra practice. But this time, you're able to recognise it as 'Timmy', take a step back, and notice the self-sabotaging thoughts you're having are just Timmy being destructive. You can think rationally about the situation – are these thoughts you want to listen to or not? You realise that doing the additional work is important and something you want to do. It aligns with your Values Compass. Therefore you choose to stay longer after one of your existing sessions, laugh at that lazy Timmy trying to take shortcuts and continue with your plan. You're not trying to get rid of Timmy, because you know that's impossible, but you can at least separate yourself from these thoughts and then give yourself more of a choice as to whether you listen to them or not.

Name your mind

You can use a metaphor to name your mind.

For example, if your mind is very bossy and stern, it might remind you of the fictional headmistress in Roald Dahl's Matilda, so you might say to yourself, 'Here's Miss Trunchbull again'. Or if

> your mind is overly pessimistic, perhaps, 'Looks like Radio Doom and Gloom has rocked up'.
>
> Or you can think about the characteristics of your Thinking Mind. Perhaps it's overly critical so Negative Nelly suits it well, or it worries about all the things that might go wrong so you might call it The Catastrophiser.
>
> Note down what you might call your pesky Thinking Mind.

Naming your mind is a simple way to get that distance from your thoughts and feelings. You can't control the thoughts that your Thinking Mind generates, but by getting that distance, you can control what actions you take (whatever thoughts your Thinking Mind comes up with)

> When talking about energy and motivation, particularly in the context of high-performance sport, it's important to learn to listen to and understand your own body. There will be times when it's beneficial to listen to those thoughts that are telling you to rest and allow time for your mind and body to recover. Pushing through extreme fatigue can cause injury and illness. Take some time to really consider if what your mind is telling you is helpful for you or not. For those of you who really struggle with listening to your body, using a coach or a training plan can be helpful so that you have guidance on what level of training you should be doing.

Accept being uncomfortable: Urge Surfing

As we've discussed in this book, all your emotions are important, and prime your body with an impulse or urge to act in a certain way. When you are feeling motivated, you may get urges to do something, for example, focus fully in a training session or match, run hard to the end line in a physical session. At times though, we can have an urge to avoid something, such as a competition or training session.

Whenever an urge arises, you have two choices: act upon it or don't act upon it.

When you are aware of an urge, you need to ask yourself: If I act on this urge, will it help me to perform my best? If the answer is yes, then it makes sense to act on that urge. For instance, 'I'm having an urge to stop the session one set early'. If you are tired and thinking about dinner already, it's probable that stopping early is just your mind trying to conserve your energy and actually acting on the urge won't help you get fitter. If, however, you've got a bad ankle and have been running through the pain, stopping before any more damage is done is probably quite a sensible solution. There is not one 'right answer' in most of these situations, it's down to you to answer those questions of yourself as honestly as you can.

When it comes to handling your urges effectively, the first step is simply to acknowledge what you're feeling. Just silently say to yourself, 'I'm having the urge to do X'.

The second step is to check in with how it will impact your performance: Will acting on this urge help me to perform at my best? If the answer is yes, then go ahead and act, using that urge to guide you and give you momentum. But if the answer is no, then instead take some action that's more in line with how you want to perform.

What should you do if you have an urge that pushes you away from performing at your best? Rather than try to resist, control or suppress it (which we know takes a lot of energy and most of the time, doesn't work), we want to practise 'urge surfing'. Have you ever sat on the beach and watched the waves? Just noticed them coming and going? A wave starts off small and builds gently. Then gradually it gathers speed and grows bigger. It continues to grow and move forward until it reaches a peak, known as a crest. Then, once the wave has crested, it gradually subsides. The same happens with urges in your body. They start off small and then steadily increase in size, before peaking and receding once again.

All too often we get into a struggle with our urges; that's why we talk of 'resisting' them. In urge surfing, though, we don't try to resist our urges – we just give them space. We *Accept Being Uncomfortable* as the urge rises and falls. If you give an ocean wave enough space, it will reach a crest and then harmlessly subside. But what happens if that wave encounters resistance? Ever seen a wave crash against the rocks? It's loud, messy and potentially destructive. Urge surfing is a simple but effective technique in which we treat our urges like waves, and 'surf' them until they dissipate.

To surf an urge rather than be 'wiped out' by it, you need to:

Urge Surfing

- Observe the urge: notice, with openness and curiosity, where you feel it in your body.
- Acknowledge: 'I'm having the urge to … X, Y, Z'.
- Breathe into it and make room for it: don't try to suppress it or get rid of it.
- Watch the urge as it rises, crests and then falls again. If difficult thoughts arise, 'thank you mind' or 'name the story' or use your preferred *Drop the Struggle* technique.

It can be helpful to score the urge on a scale of 1 to 10. For example, 'I'm having the urge to X, and it's now a 7'. Keep checking in on the urge: noticing whether it's rising, peaking or falling. Remember, no matter how huge that urge gets, you have room for it. And if you give it enough space, then sooner or later it will crest and then subside. Observe it, breathe into it, open up around it, make lots of space and allow it to come and go in its own good time.

At the same time, check in with how you want to perform. Ask yourself, 'What action can I take right now – instead of trying to resist or control my urges – that will help me perform at my best?' Then whatever the answer is – go ahead and do it.

Practising this away from sport can then help you to take this mentality back to the pitch, or boat, or court or whatever your arena. When you are noticing dips in motivation, just acknowledge it, allow them to be there, but continue to behave in a way that you know will help you perform the way you can perform. The last step in this chapter will also help you with this.

Play in the now: Move in slow motion

When we think about motivation, we typically think about it in terms of future goals – where we want to get to. Clearly, to be the best you can be in your sport, these future goals are key. But, just as important is the ability to be present, because it's being present that allows us to carry out the actions that help us get to where we want to get to.

Rather than ignoring or shying away from feeling demotivated, it helps to open ourselves fully to it. Exploring the sensations, thoughts and emotions that arise when we feel resistance to do something will increase our awareness and a sense of acceptance to the fact that we are having difficulties with motivation. Being more present allows us a chance to explore obstacles and give ourselves a sense of space in choosing how we want to respond.

A great way to practise the mindfulness needed to be present, is to do things at half speed.

Doing things at half speed

The steps are simple:

- Step 1: Pick an activity.
- Step 2: Do it at half speed.

That's it. No sitting down. No closing your eyes. No quiet environment away from noise. Just you, here and now, at half the speed.

You can practise whilst taking a shower. Step into the shower as if moving in slow motion, and then slowly turn the knob. Feel the water droplets on your skin and the change in temperature. Now pick up the shampoo bottle, and slowly massage the shampoo into your hair.

You can practise whilst eating your breakfast. Slowly pick up a spoon, and press it gently into your food. Lift it up and then slowly take the first bite. Take your time to chew and then consciously swallow. Whenever you do an activity in slow motion, you automatically notice more facets of your experience, more of the richness and complexity even of simple actions.

Your attention naturally shifts as you slow down. You can make space for whatever thoughts and feelings you are having. You will probably notice an urge to move more quickly, and maybe even some self-doubts like 'This is stupid' or 'This is not working'. That's fine. Notice these urges and thoughts, and then continue in slow motion. You may want to challenge yourself to move in slow motion for 30 seconds. Then one minute. And then maybe even three minutes. It's your choice.

By moving in slow motion, you will learn to bring your attention to your present experience and practise a skillset necessary to disentangle from difficult thoughts and emotions. Whenever you get caught up in your own head, notice what you are doing, and refocus on the here and now. That way you have the space to choose to do the actions that move you towards being the athlete you want to be.

What's in your kitbag?

Values are your inner compass, helping you to set off on and stay on the path towards performing well and getting the most from your sport and your life. At times we can forget about our values, things get in the way and try to steer us off path. But values are intrinsic in nature and are more sustainable in the long run than extrinsic sources of motivation, such as a gold medal. One of the best kitbag skills to build and keep your motivation is to pick up your Values Compass and remind yourself of what it is that's important to you.

Even with a clear Values Compass, day-to-day slumps in energy and motivation are common. We avoid things, procrastinate or opt out of things we know deep down will take us in the direction we want to go. Getting into a routine of small, simple and easy-to-do habits – rather than always focussing on the end goal – will help you to *Do What Matters*. You will focus your energy and behaviour on the things that are important to you and take you in the direction you want to go in.

There will be times when action isn't enough. You will need your kitbag of exercises to address your thoughts and feelings directly:

- Giving your mind a name helps you remember your thoughts are just thoughts, so you can *Drop the Struggle* with them

- Surfing an urge keeps you motivated and on track as you *Accept Being Uncomfortable*

- Practising daily actions in slow motion helps you to be present and *Play in the Now.*

Together they allow thoughts and feelings to be there without negatively impacting your life or performance when your energy has slumped.

Let's examine the final challenge of setbacks and failure next in Chapter 8.

Chapter 8

Embrace setbacks and failure

Embrace your losses as fair payment for the surplus of being alive.
KIERAN SETIYA

Sometimes we fall into the trap of thinking that life should be straightforward, we ask ourselves 'Why me?' when something bad happens and we resent situations or people that we don't want or like. Of course, we know life isn't all positive, but we still find it hard to deal with setbacks when they arise. Experiencing setbacks is part of what it means to be an athlete. The nature of sport is inherently up and down. So it's our ability to stay on track, maintain our focus and make space for the uncomfortable feelings that is most important in our journey to becoming the person and performer we want to be.

Setbacks are to learn from

In Japan, they have a method of repairing broken pottery called 'Kintsugi'. It involves fixing broken items and transforming them into a new work of art with gold. The scars and cracks of the broken ceramic become the focus and turn the object from something broken into something unique and exquisite. As a philosophy, it treats breakage and repair as part of the history of an object, rather than something to disguise.

There's a lot we can learn from this in the way that we respond to our own failure, setbacks and adversity.

It's easy to assume that achieving great things in your sport, such as making it to an Olympics, means you'll never face or grapple with a setback. However, a study of British Olympians who competed at the 2016 Games, found that even being able to perform at the highest level does not protect you from the emotional lows of setbacks. The athletes who failed to meet their performance expectations in Rio experienced a variety of emotions including anxiety, crying and interpersonal hypersensitivity. These feelings were compounded when their failure resulted in a sudden loss of 'celebrity' status and by family members who did not fully understand the ups and downs associated with the demands of an Olympic campaign. It seems setbacks are hard even for Olympians.[1]

Unfortunately, setbacks can take us away from the direction that we want to go in and make us feel inadequate or like we've failed. But they can also be a powerful and important part of developing as an athlete. With the benefit of hindsight, we can come to view setbacks as a necessary part of our lives. Research shows us that having the opportunity to learn from failure can turn it into a positive experience that satisfies reward centres in the brain.[2]

In addition, science shows that experiencing some setbacks and adversity can have beneficial sporting outcomes. Olympic gold medalists and world champions claim that setbacks such as repeated non-selection, significant sporting failure, serious injury, political unrest and the loss of a family member were a key part of their psychological and performance development.[3] Experience of adversity can be important for sporting success. Many of these high-level athletes believed that if they had not experienced certain types of stressors at specific times, they would not have won their gold medals.

Drop the struggle: I am not my story

When we have a setback, it's so easy to rush into believing we are a failure, a loser, a rubbish athlete and generally that we're not good enough to succeed and achieve our dream outcome. In our minds we go around this spiral of thinking over and over again: uncomfortable thoughts and feelings bubble up when we lose, don't get selected or make a mistake. We focus on protecting and maintaining our self-esteem, hold on tightly to a narrow self-story and beat ourselves up because we haven't met our inflated standards compared with other people.

That's our Thinking Mind at work.

In Chapter 1, you learnt how to use your Observing Mind to get some perspective on your internal experiences, that the 'who I am' is not the sum of your experiences. The fact you weren't selected doesn't define who you are as a person. When your training partner beats you in a race, that doesn't change who you are as an athlete.

Building that strong and open sense of self isn't a one-off. It will be challenged every time you face a setback. Here's an exercise that uses your Observing Mind to help you have a much broader self-story to take into training and competition.

I am / I am not[4]

In your notebook, write down these three sentences.

1. I am _____
2. I am _____
3. I am _____

1. Think about a recent setback you've experienced, for example, failing to achieve a personal best, being dropped from the team, being beaten by someone who ranks lower than you. Complete the top two statements with one-word answers that represent positive psychological attributes of yours that you still think are true (not just descriptive things like 'I am tall', 'I am male'). Refer to your favourite qualities about yourself. This might be 'I am determined', 'I am capable', 'I am brave' and so on.

For the last statement, do the exact opposite – on the back of the setback, write down a personal attribute you think you have that is negative. This might be 'I am weak', 'I am a loser', 'I am rubbish', 'I am anxious' and so on.

2. Let's begin by reviewing the top two 'positive' answers.

I have a simple question for you to think about: is this true, all of the time, everywhere and towards everyone, without exception?

Now, ask yourself the same for the bottom one. Is this true, all of the time, everywhere and towards everyone, without exception?

Most likely, you will realise that the answer to both of these questions is no. You are those things, but not all of the time. Especially with negative self-judgements, our minds can convince us that we are those things, all of the time.

3. Now see how many of these statements you can turn into a comparison with other people. If you wrote 'I am brave' then add ER to the sentence so it becomes 'I am brav-ER', or weak becomes 'I am weak-ER' and so on. Notice that suddenly this isn't just your story of failure, it's your story of failure compared with other athletes. No wonder this feels uncomfortable.

4. Then take each sentence and add a comma at the end and add the words 'or not'. For example 'I am brave, or not'. Try this with all three words.

Read each sentence slowly and watch what happens. If you find your critical Thinking Mind pops up here, use the skills you have learnt so far in Chapter 3 to unhook, such as saying, 'I am noticing ... I am having the thought that ...'.

You may find a little loosening here, with more space or more options. Don't hold too tight to any feelings that come up – whatever they are they will come and go – and don't get into an argument with yourself about which version is more accurate. You now realise that you can choose the 'version' of yourself that you pay attention to. Try to open your mind to the possibility that there are other ways of thinking about yourself on the back of this setback.

5. Finally, take the first sentence and cross out all the things you have written after 'I am'. Who would you be without that content? Pause a moment to reflect on that. Then do the same with the other two sentences. Imagine how you might act or behave if you just let go of all that content. In the face of this setback, who are you without the stories you are telling yourself? How might you run, jump or play if you could do it, just as yourself? Read out the words 'I am' a few times – picture what you might be doing if you could simply play your sport just as you are. How refreshing is that.

The aim of this exercise is to help you build a more flexible story of who you are as an athlete. Keep reminding yourself of this when you catch yourself being overly judgemental in the face of a setback or when things don't go as planned. That way you can *Drop the Struggle* with the thoughts swishing round your head. You realise that setbacks are part of the journey, and you are still amazing, just as you are. This won't change the setback happening, and it might not change setbacks that happen in the future, but it will change how you feel about yourself in the midst of something going wrong. And that, in effect, changes everything.

Accept being uncomfortable: The discomfort of setbacks

Nobody wants to face setbacks. In 1976, on his way to a second World Championship Title in Formula One racing, Niki Lauda hit a little bump in the road; he was wiped out during a race.[5] His car burst into flames, skidded back out onto the track and was broadsided by another car. Lauda got torched inside his Ferrari; much of his face was incinerated before he was pulled to safety. He bled internally and lapsed into a coma. It was touch and go for a few days, but Lauda pulled through. Forty-three days later, he was behind the wheel at the Italian Grand Prix. Lauda would go on to win two more championship titles before retiring.

It seemed like a fairytale ending to a horrific accident. But Lauda openly spoke not just about the physical challenges of returning to the sport he loved, but the mental gremlins he battled. He was gripped with fear and anxiety as he got back into his car, saying 'suddenly the whole crash overtook me. I panicked, I was afraid and couldn't make it'. Thankfully he took himself away and focussed on what was important to him. That enabled him to overcome the discomfort of his situation and to drive again.

Lauda's story is an amazing one, but setbacks don't automatically lead to better outcomes in the future. There are also a lot of examples of people who struggle after a setback, and whose lives and sport are negatively impacted.

So, what's the difference?

We believe one of the key differences is the ability to recognise setbacks as a normal, natural and necessary part of life and sport. Once you can see failure and setbacks like that, you become more willing to experience them. Think back to Chapter 4 where you explored how to *Accept Being Uncomfortable* with strong thoughts and feelings. As you become better at doing this, the fear of failure doesn't need to rule you. You are more willing to step into the risks that come with pushing yourself into new situations, including the risk of not succeeding.

The story of the yellowtail moth explains this beautifully.

The yellowtail moth

One sunny day an old woman found a cocoon of a yellowtail moth. Being curious about how this papery shell could transform into a moth, she took it home. She sat and waited for the yellowtail moth to emerge from the cocoon. As she waited patiently, she noticed the moth battling its way to force its body through a tiny little hole in the cocoon. Then unexpectedly it seemed to stop making any progress. It appeared as if the moth could go no further. It just seemed to be stuck.

Then the woman, being kind, decided to help the moth. So she took a pair of scissors and snipped off the remaining bit of the cocoon. The moth then emerged easily. But it had a swollen body and small, shrivelled wings. She expected that the wings would enlarge and expand to be able to support the body which would contract in time. Neither happened. In fact, the little moth spent the rest of its short life crawling around with a swollen body and shrivelled wings. It never was able to fly.

What the woman in her kindness and haste did not understand was that uncomfortableness of the restricting cocoon and the work required for the moth to get through the tiny opening, forced fluid from the moth's body into its wings – and that meant it would be healthy and ready for flight once it achieved its free-dom from the cocoon. Freedom and flight would only come after the challenge of emerging from the cocoon.

Life and sport are challenging. We all face issues that are arduous and demanding – setbacks, selection, confidence, injury, loss of form, anxiety and relationships to name just a few. But being able to accept that setbacks come with uncomfortable thoughts and feelings can completely change your relationship with them and give you a greater level of strength going forward.

Next time you experience a setback or failure, see how you can shift your mindset to view it as a natural part of striving towards success. It may be helpful at this point to go back to Chapter 4 and pull out one of the exercises to practise.

Play in the now: Drop anchor

It's easy to get caught up in all-consuming thoughts about failure. We often find ourselves catastrophising about what will happen to us as a result of a setback. It can make us feel anxious and lose confidence in ourselves and what we can do in the future. Whilst it's not always possible to be present, at times when you need it, it can really help. This activity is one of our favourites and works no matter who you are or what mind state you are in. Set some time aside to give it a go.

When you are pulled around by critical or judgemental thoughts try-ing to tell you you're a failure, or your life is over, it's a bit like being tossed around in a storm. You can't think or act effectively. You'll keep cycling through these thoughts and behaviours until you can regain some awareness and control over what's happening. This is where the drop anchor comes in.

The drop anchor[6] exercise will allow you to centre yourself, take control of your arms, legs and body, so you can focus and get on with doing what's important at this moment. It is easy to get caught up in thoughts and feelings, for example, 'I'm useless', 'I'll never be any good', 'There's no point' and so on. You are not trying to get rid of the thoughts – they are perfectly normal. This exercise helps bring you into the now and concentrate on taking the next step.

Drop Anchor

To play this as a recording, go to https://www.yellowtailgroup.co.uk/team-4

- Push your feet hard into the floor. Feel the ground beneath you.
- Stand up straight/sit up straight. Notice how you are standing/sitting.
- Push your hands firmly together.
- As well as these thoughts/feelings/memories, notice your body – notice your hands, feet, back.
- Take a few moments to notice your breath, in and out. You don't need to change it, simply notice it.
- Also look around the room and notice five things you can see.
- And also notice three things you can hear.
- And also notice you and anyone working around you, united, working together

So there are thoughts, feelings, memories here ….

And your body.
And the room around you.
And you are working together right here right now.

Make the exercise last as long as needed to ground you. It could take one minute, ten minutes or more depending on how caught up in your thoughts you are.

It's important to continue acknowledging the presence of the unhelpful thoughts and feelings, otherwise this will turn into a distraction technique rather than a way to unhook you from your thoughts and feelings and focus on the now.

Do what matters: Go in the right direction

It's very easy to get knocked off track when setbacks come along. In Chapter 3 we explored the ways we do this. Go back to your list of ways that you distract yourself when things get tough. It could be you take your mind off the setback by overtraining, opting out of important activities such as key matches or events or wasting lots of energy by going over and over the setback, blaming yourself, thinking it's not fair, figuring out why it happened and so on.

Ninety seven metres below sea level is perhaps an odd place for Sofía Gómez Uribe to find herself given she was born in the Colombian mountain town of Pereira. Gómez is a Columbian freediver, holding six national records, setting several world records along the way and culminating, in September 2018, with a world record. But in 2019 she suffered a major setback. As she explained:

'I think during 2019 I was a little bit overwhelmed with competitions and then I had an injury, a lung squeeze. Many freedivers don't think that lung squeezes are important or serious but that made me rethink what I wanted to do as a freediver'.

So Gómez took time out of the sport to try to reconnect with the sport she loved. Her way of overcoming the setback was, 'I don't want to put pressure on myself, that I have to do a record or that I have to be the best. I want to enjoy it and to fall in love again with going deep and with competing … And of course my dream is to go deeper than 100 metres … But because I love it, not because I have to'.

Two years later she returned to one of the most highly anticipated events on the competitive freediving calendar: Vertical Blue 2022. Called the 'Wimbledon of Freediving', it is the most prestigious invitational freediving competition on the planet. Held at Dean's Blue Hole, a 202-metre-deep freediving destination in the Bahamas. She emerged from the week-long event in third place, her setback a thing of the past. Who knows if she will achieve her dream of going below 100 metres, but we do know Gómez has taken the first step to overcome her setback.[7]

We imagine, like Gómez, you want to find it in yourself to get back on track and overcome failure and setbacks.

We've learnt in Chapters 6 and 7 that confidence and motivation are as much actions as they are feelings. The same can be said for overcoming setbacks. One of the best ways to overcome setbacks is to take action – action that takes us towards what's important to us and that will lead us in the direction we want to go.

Let's use the 'doing what matters matrix'[8] here.

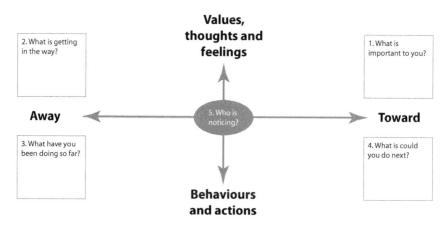

Values, thoughts and feelings

2. What is getting in the way?

1. What is important to you?

Away ← 5. Who is noticing? → **Toward**

3. What have you been doing so far?

4. What is could you do next?

Behaviours and actions

Doing what matters matrix

The 'doing what matters matrix' brings together your thoughts and feelings and your actions to help you step forward after a setback.

The next time you experience a setback, set aside a few minutes to complete this exercise.

To start with, copy the 'doing what matters' matrix pictured above, and write down your answers to these four questions.

1. What's important to you?

Despite the setback, what do you appreciate and value that you most want to walk towards? What qualities do you want to demonstrate right now? For example, the thought you are making a difference, the joy you get from running races or the pleasure of being in a team. The values work you did in Chapter 5 might help you with this.

2. What's getting in the way?

Now let's think about the thoughts and feelings when you are caught up in the setback. What thoughts and feelings move you in the opposite direction to where you want to go or how you want to be, such as resentment about not being picked, embarrassment about coming last, feeling that you are not good enough.

3. What have you been doing so far?

Now move to your actions and behaviours. When you are moving away from the things you want, what are you doing? This might be dodging training, being hesitant in a game, getting angry at yourself or your coach.

4. **What could you do next?**

Then, staying with your actions and behaviour, when you are moving in your chosen direction, what are you doing? Such as, committing to practise, doing your weights session, really listening to the coach, making confident moves on the pitch.

Finally, on the matrix, look at where the two lines intersect and notice who is noticing the answers you've written. That's your Observing Mind that can notice all that's going on. Remind yourself that you can choose which direction you are going in next, in spite of the setback.

The matrix is a tool to put in your kitbag and revisit when setbacks happen, whether they are small or large. When you need to *Do What Matters* and take action, you can bring it to mind, jog around the quadrants, updating as you go with tweaks that fit the current situation – you get to choose which direction you go.

What's in your kitbag?

Sport doesn't just come with the ups, there are also the downs to contend with. Setbacks are unwanted situations in life that can make you feel inadequate or like you've failed. No one wants to have a setback, but the harsh reality is they will happen throughout your life and as an athlete. To be a high-performing individual, learning to deal with setbacks is a powerful and important part of fulfilling your potential.

In this chapter you used some of the tools you learnt earlier in the book, as well as added some more to your kitbag:

- Knowing you are not the story you tell yourself, about yourself, equips you to *Drop the Struggle* with your thoughts and realise you are amazing just as you are.

- The yellowtail moth reminds you to *Accept Being Uncomfortable* with the challenges that come with setbacks and difficulties.

- Dropping anchor allows you to *Play in the Now* so you can step back from your frustration or sadness.

- Using the doing what matters matrix encourages you to take forward action and *Do What Matters*.

All these exercises help you to stay on track, maintain your focus and make space for the uncomfortable feelings that inevitably arise when things don't go as planned.

In Chapter 9, let's finish packing your kitbag for the journey ahead so you can explore what you are capable of and fulfil your dreams as an athlete.

Chapter *9*

The onward journey

Sometimes that smallest step in the right direction ends up being the biggest step of your life. Tiptoe if you must, but take a step.
NAEEM CALLAWAY

At the start of this book, we promised to be your guides as you climbed the mountain to improve your sport performance. We've called out directions and suggested new pathways. In your kitbag you have some tools to navigate the terrain, lead you out of dead ends and to keep on climbing. We still can't do the climbing for you, nor know what it feels like on your mountain, but we hope you now see where you are about to step and have more choices about the different routes you can take as you ascend your mountain.

Enjoy the journey

Although we've come to the end of this book, it's only the beginning of your journey using all the skills, tools and processes that we've given you. Whether you started reading this book yesterday or a year ago, we hope that you're less likely to be pushed around by those thoughts and feelings that hold you back and get in the way of enjoying and succeeding at your sport.

We've no idea which mountains you'll climb, or where you'll end up. And the truth is, nor do you. Life is unexpected. What we do know is, in trying and practising the tools in your new kitbag, you've learnt how to think and act flexibly. That means you can adapt over time and as your circumstances change.

For example, maybe you've already applied the tools in this book to the biggest issue you are facing in sport at the moment, such as selection to the premier league side or competing in a major tournament. But what if you're unexpectedly injured, and suddenly a feeling of anxiety, that you've never had before, comes up? You are so caught up in your thoughts you can't focus and are avoiding putting in the rehab work to get back fit. What you've learnt will help you with this or any other new situation.

Whatever the challenge, use the:

- *Play in the Now* tools to get present and be mindful, so you can focus on what's important

- *Drop the Struggle* with difficult thoughts and feelings like 'I'm not good enough' or the 'What if ...' stories that keep coming up, so they don't take energy from what's really important

- *Accept Being Uncomfortable*, realising the difficult thoughts and feelings are part of your experience as an athlete, so they don't get in the way of doing the important things

- *Do What Matters*, so you actually go and do what's most important to you as an athlete and live in line with your values.

Don't worry too much about which of these tools you pull out of your kitbag first and in which order. They all work together – a bit like a coach, strength and conditioning advisor, physiotherapist, psychologist and nutritionist work together to help you to perform better. Sometimes one is more helpful than another, but in the end you need them all to succeed.

Armed with these tools to help you on the onward journey, we have two more additional items to pack in your kitbag.

Developing the flexibility to successfully face each day and the situations that you come across is always ongoing (and in fact is a lifelong process). It's hard. Despite what you now know, you may still get easily pulled off track by situations that cause all your difficult thoughts and feelings to come rushing back.

The Choice Point is our 'go to' kitbag tool in these situations. It enables us to choose to be the athlete we want to be and participate in our sport in a way that's meaningful to us. The Choice Point is a tool that combines everything we've learnt in this book – our ability to notice all that's going on for us *and* to *Play in the Now, Drop the Struggle, Accept Being Uncomfortable* and *Do What Matters.* When you combine The Choice Point with our final tool, a dose of kindness or self-compassion, it is so much easier to get back on track and focus on doing all the important things you love to do to perform well again.

Choose to stay on track with The Choice Point

It's easy to act confidently, overcome setbacks, deal with pressure, be motivated or focus on your goals when things are easy – when we do a training session that's well within our capability, playing in a squad where we are the best player, competing against a team that's inexperienced and so on.

But once you put this book down, every day you will face more challenging situations – learning a new skill, entering a bigger competition, being selected for a different team or being the new member of a squad.

In each of these situations, you have a choice. Do you:

- Do what's important to you, what takes you towards your sporting dream and the life you want to live as an athlete? OR

- Wait until you feel confident, happy, certain, calm, motivated or unlikely to fail, moving away from acting like the athlete you want to be?

Let's use The Choice Point. Grab your notebook and a pen and let's draw this out together.[1]

All day long we do things – make breakfast, go for a run, practise our sport, talk with friends, watch a clip of the opposition; we're even doing something as we recover sleeping in bed.

Some things we do move us towards the life we want as an athlete – training hard, recovering well, being kind, spending time talking to the coach (i.e. behaving like the athlete we want to be) – we call these 'towards moves'.

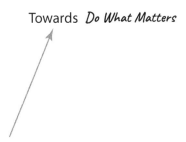

Towards *Do What Matters*

Some things we do move us away from the life we want to live – giving up, avoiding tough situations, not practising, being rude (i.e. not behaving like the athlete we want to be) – we call these 'away moves'.

For example, think back to the story of Usain Bolt in Chapter 6 for a moment. Given his desire to become multiple Olympic Champion and his values of dedication and commitment, giving 100% to a session, doing his mobility exercises and drinking his protein shakes would all be 'towards moves'. Staying up late, missing a physio appointment to play Xbox and bingeing on McDonalds would probably be 'away moves'.

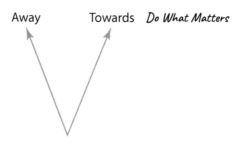

Now when life is easy, giving us what we want, it is usually fairly simple for us to choose towards moves – to act confidently, be motivated, stay focussed and to do the things that help us to improve our sport performance in the long term. In Chapter 5, you learnt how to *Do What Matters* by identifying the core values that act as your compass for being an athlete. Remind yourself of your Values Compass now. When you act on these values, what things do you do in your sport? How would you train, perform or compete differently, how would you behave towards others differently, how would you talk to yourself differently and so on? Add these actions to your choice point. They give you a clear idea of the sort of athlete you are when you are doing a 'towards move'.

Unfortunately, life and sport aren't that easy – and don't give us what we want a lot of the time. Performing well as an athlete can be hard. We face challenging situations that dent our confidence, make us nervous, take us off track, cause us to doubt our capability and so on. As a result, lots of difficult thoughts and feelings come up for us. Maybe we focus on all the things that might go wrong, or worry about embarrassing ourselves or say really judgemental and critical things to ourselves.

Now think about a situation that is challenging you right now, whether you're competing or training. Choose one challenging situation you are facing and add that to your Choice Point. Add the thoughts and feelings that go with this situation. Remember in Chapter 1 we explored some of the ways your time-travelling Thinking Mind pulls you off track such as:

- Coming up with reasons you can't ... or giving you excuses

- Judging you negatively

- Telling you that you must look good or be right

- Striving for perfection

- Crippling you with anxiety, fear, sadness, anger, shame, guilt and so on

- Insisting that 'You can't be any good if you feel ...'

- Following the urge to overtrain, restrict your diet, drink too much and so on

Do What Matters

Away   Towards   e.g. being **courageous** in matches to go for interceptions
e.g. **committing** to training 100% and completing the programme

Challenging Situations,
Thoughts & Feelings

e.g. Situation = Going for 1ˢᵗ team selection
Thoughts = 'I don't have what it takes?', 'I'm going to mess things up?'
Feelings = 'I feel so anxious and my palms are sweaty'

And we learnt in Chapters 2, 3 and 4, it is easy to keep struggling with these difficult thoughts and feelings. We avoid situations that make us feel uncomfortable and spend lots of time worrying about what might happen or just did happen. The thoughts and feelings reel us in, pull us around and send us off track.

And once we are struggling with our thoughts and feelings, we start doing away moves. These could range from avoiding training or ignoring our own needs, to not committing to our team or doing things that don't support our health or relationships. Add to The Choice Point the 'away moves' that you do when you are in these challenging situations.

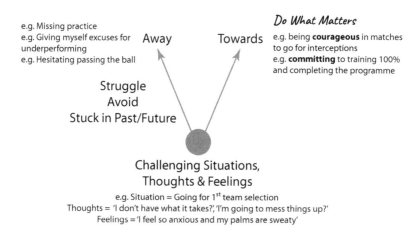

Now you could stay doing away moves and not fulfil your potential. But you now have a full kitbag of ways to unhook yourself from these unhelpful thoughts and feelings. Pick your favourites. For example, using your Observing Mind to notice them, you could use the exercise

Lemon, Lemon, Lemon to *Drop the Struggle*. You could turn off the struggle switch to *Accept Being Uncomfortable*. And you could take a mindful breath to become present and *Play in the Now*. That way you make 'towards' moves and *Do What Matters* instead – doing the things that move you towards the athlete you want to be, getting the best from your performance. And the better you get at this, the more you fulfil your sports potential.

Away   Towards *Do What Matters*

Struggle
Avoid
Stuck in past/future

Drop the Struggle
Accept Being Uncomfortable
Play in the Now

Challenging Situations,
Thoughts & Feelings

Glenmore's choice point example

A cricketer we worked with identified his 'away moves'. Pre-season, when he was on a run, he often got an urge to start walking. This happened particularly when he reached a hill. His Thinking Mind went 'You're not fit enough to make it up this hill, just walk' and other thoughts might pop into his head like 'it doesn't even matter if you run or not, just save yourself the hard work'. He also didn't enjoy the feeling of being out of breath. For a long time, he would struggle with these thoughts and feelings, and either used every ounce of motivation he had to push through (which sometimes worked but often didn't), or gave in to them and walked.

We encouraged him to open his kitbag and take out a tool. For Glenmore it was a total game-changer when he learnt to just watch these thoughts, and not buy into them. He'd do this typically by singing them to himself in a random tune as he

continued running with a smile on his face, laughing at how ridic-
ulous he was and hoping that no one came around the corner!

He also practised surfing the urge to stop as soon as his breathing became a little laboured. He acknowledged that his breathing
was uncomfortable as he ran up the hill, noticing it with curiosity
and making space for it as he continued to climb on his run.

One of our favourite ways to *Drop the Struggle* is to start by thanking
our mind. If you use this, then whatever your mind says to you, no matter
how mean or hurtful it is, just say 'Thanks mind, thanks for sharing' with
a sense of humour. You can let your mind prattle on, whilst you focus
your attention on things that you want to do. Make sure you do this
with a sense of playfulness, as it's essentially a way of not taking your
thoughts too seriously.

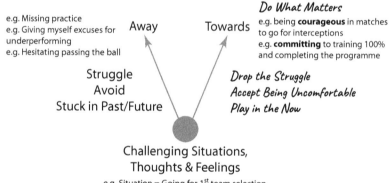

Do What Matters

e.g. Missing practice
e.g. Giving myself excuses for   Away   Towards   e.g. being **courageous** in matches
underperforming   to go for interceptions
e.g. Hesitating passing the ball   e.g. **committing** to training 100%
                                                          and completing the programme

Struggle   *Drop the Struggle*
Avoid   *Accept Being Uncomfortable*
Stuck in Past/Future   *Play in the Now*

Challenging Situations,
Thoughts & Feelings
e.g. Situation = Going for 1st team selection
Thoughts = 'I don't have what it takes?', 'I'm going to mess things up?'
Feelings = 'I feel so anxious and my palms are sweaty'

Then look in the kitbag you have just packed and remind yourself of
your favourite tools to help you *Accept Being Uncomfortable* and *Play
in the Now*. Add these to your Choice Point – they are your 'go to' tools
when you are struggling.

Next time you find yourself grappling with a difficult situation,
remember you always have a choice about what you do and how
you respond (that's why this tool is called The Choice Point). How you
respond is up to you.

You can struggle and get caught up with your thoughts and feelings, make away moves that stop you from acting confidently, being motivated and focussed and prevent you from playing your sport in the way you want to. You can wait until you feel confident before you play/run/jump/cycle/swim like the athlete you want to be.

Or you can *Drop the Struggle* with the thoughts and feelings that come up. After all, you've learnt by now that you have little control over these thoughts and feelings. However, you do have control over being the sports person you want to be and the steps you take towards your dreams and goals. Make space for those uncomfortable thoughts and feelings as you *Accept Being Uncomfortable. Play in the Now* by being mindful in this moment and the next. Whatever the situation, you now have the tools in your kitbag to achieve this. And choose to *Do What Matters* by taking small steps followed by larger confident steps towards your dream. Who knows what you'll achieve.

A dose of self-compassion when things don't go to plan

After reading this book, you will know all the things you need to do to become the person and the athlete you want to be. You've got the understanding, the self-awareness and the tools to take you further in sport and life.

The reality is, however, that you won't do everything you've learnt in this book. You'll forget, do it wrong, get impatient and maybe even give up.

Regardless of where you are on this journey, it's important to remember that not every day will be perfect. Balancing the desire to improve with an understanding that this is an ongoing journey is important. Progress won't be linear. You'll make gains one week and then struggle another week. You may even go backwards one week – this is normal, you are only human. The same is true for life, it's not linear, and there will be bumps along the road.

What you need in these moments is not to beat yourself up, or question yourself over and over again whether you are doing enough, or doing things right.

It's self-compassion.

Self-compassion, put simply, is being kind to yourself. Rather than beating yourself up, wishing you were different, it's accepting you are only human and that you can't be perfect all the time. It's treating yourself with kindness.

Pause for a moment if you're reading this thinking, 'being self-critical helps me to motivate myself. It makes me do things that I can't be bothered to do, because I feel so bad about myself'. At the start of this book, we told you that the techniques we will teach you aim to have a sustained, long-lasting impact. Being self-critical, over time, is not a positive motivator. It will not help you to be the person and performer you want to be.

Imagine that you have a donkey. You bought your donkey to help you carry your heavy bags. Now, you can motivate your donkey with a stick, every time he looks like he's going to stop, you give him a whack with your big stick, and he carries on again. Performance output is probably positive – he will carry your load. But, more likely than not, you will end up with a battered bruised donkey that feels aggrieved. It might work for a few weeks, even months, but at some point that donkey is going to say 'I've had enough'.

Another option is to motivate your donkey with carrots. You are kind and encouraging towards your donkey, letting him rest when he needs to, but positively encouraging him to keep going when he gets tired. Performance output will be the same, but this time you'll most likely end up with a happier, healthier donkey.

Use this metaphor to think about how you treat yourself. Are you beating yourself up, which seems to work in the short term, but is likely to have a long-term cost? Or can you respond to yourself with kindness and self-compassion, encouragement and generosity?

Another way to think about it is how you would treat a friend.

When your closest friend is not at their best, has failed at something or needs support, what would you say to them? Would you tell them they're useless and lazy and don't deserve all the things they've achieved? They might as well give up. Or would you be encouraging, positive and reassure them that you will be with them every step of the way?

I think we all know what the right answer is here. The truth is, we can often be very self-critical, judgemental and intolerant of anything less than perfection when it comes to ourselves. But we also have the choice and ability to show ourselves kindness, compassion and patience.

Since you are with yourself 24/7, what kind of friend do you want to be to yourself?

Pack your kitbag

It's over to you now to use the tools you have learnt.

Go back through the book and reflect on the most impactful chapters, exercises, metaphors and tools. Take some time here to record in your notebook those you'd like to add to your new kitbag. You could draw yourself a table like this one.

When I need to ...	Where to look ...	I'll put in my kitbag ...
Drop the Struggle	Chapters 3, 6, 7, 8	
Accept Being Uncomfortable	Chapters 4, 6, 7, 8	
Play in the Now	Chapters 2, 6, 7, 8	
Do What Matters	Chapters 5, 6, 7, 8	

A kitbag needs to be used. It won't help your performance if you forget to take it with you to training or don't open it when you get into the sports arena. One way to make use of the content of your kitbag is to use it as part of your regular training. For example, you might decide to practise like this:

Monday – *Thinking and Observing Mind Day* – for example, I'll practise using my Observing Mind to notice what my Thinking Mind is saying about the next competition, the obstacles, self-judgements, comparisons with other people and predictions about what might happen that it's coming up with.

Tuesday – *Drop the Struggle Day* – for example, I'll practise singing my thoughts when I have to do the last few interval sessions on the hills and my mind is telling me I'm slow.

Wednesday – *Accept Being Uncomfortable Day* – for example, I'll practise saying 'yes' to any thoughts in my mind or feelings in my body that I notice.

Thursday – *Play in the Now Day* – for example, I'll practise mindfully walking from the bus to training and back.

Friday – *Do What Matters Day* – for example, I'll practise choosing one of my values and taking one tiny action that helps me live that value today.

Saturday – *My Performance Challenge Day* – for example, I'll take a challenge that I'm currently facing as an athlete such as overcoming a setback, handling a pressure situation, performing confidently or increasing my energy, and practise one thing from my kitbag that will improve my performance.

Sunday – *Recovery Day* – Put your feet up!

Time to dream big

Krista Pärmäkoski, the Finnish cross-country skier, imagined what her future might be, 'Already at the age of seven, I wrote an essay that my dream would be to become a skier. The same dream has guided me ever since.'[2] Although Pärmäkoski has five Olympic and seven world championship medals to her name, she continues to dream big. Her motivation comes from doing something that's important to her and that she loves. In her words, 'I just needed to find the simplest reasons why I love sports and focus on them. I love the feeling after training, I love the possibility to do sports as a job and I love racing against other top athletes!' She continues to imagine 'what still might be' and to dream.

Back at the beginning of this book, you probably sensed in our stories that we both had big dreams when it came to sport.

Jenna always dreamt of achieving big things. Through hockey, she set about dedicating much of her time to fulfilling her potential and becoming the best hockey player she could be. But things got in the way, motivation dipped, direction was lost and she ended up drifting through what should have been her peak. There was a period when Jenna wasn't sure of her values, what she wanted her life to be about. But she always knew that she could stretch herself to do great things. She worked out how to *Do What Matters*. Over time, this ambition shifted from great things on the hockey pitch to great things in the academic realm. It shifted from dedication to training physically, to studying, learning and developing as a sports psychology practitioner. It shifted from focussing on self-development to focussing on helping other people develop. Ultimately, her world became about helping others transform their mindset by being able to *Drop the Struggle* with what was holding them back. Jenna has now had an opportunity to work with national sports teams and GB athletes in a variety of sports, business leaders from global companies and school children who aspire to do great things themselves. It's not the life she perhaps first imagined, but by not giving up on her dreams, Jenna has developed herself and others in ways that are far better than she could have ever imagined.

As a young woman, Alison dreamt of going to the Olympics. She'd lie awake and play through what it would be like, the crowds, the medal, the setting. She thought she'd compete at the Olympics one day as a sprinter, but that's not quite how her story ends.

As a runner, she'd never heard of sport psychology or benefitted from working on her mind. She struggled with her thoughts, and let her mind tell her the 'I am not good enough story' many times. Buying into the story, Alison often felt overwhelmed with the feelings of anxiety before a race, trying everything to get rid of that feeling until she eventually stopped competing altogether. But she never gave up on the dream. Sport was her passion. Following her values of courage, excitement and authenticity, aged 43, she re-trained and went on to study for a PhD in the psychology of elite performance. She learnt how to *Drop the Struggle* with her 'I am not good enough story', to *Accept Being Uncomfortable* with the feelings of being the least knowledgeable in her class, to *Play in the Now* by staying present as she sat in lectures or wrote an essay and focussed on *Doing What Matters* in terms of studying and practise.

Although it's true, Alison never competed at the Olympics herself; she has now spent over 20 years as a psychologist walking alongside many coaches and athletes to enable them to achieve local, national, world and Olympic glory.

Neither of us stopped imagining. Imagining what a full life could be. Imagining what we would do differently if we weren't caught up in the struggles with our mind.

So our final gift to you is to imagine.

Imagine.

You go to sleep tonight and you wake up tomorrow morning. And in the night a miracle happened and all your dreams came true.

All the difficult thoughts and feelings that have held you back in sport have lost their power, like water off a duck's back, and you are the best possible version of yourself.

1. What will you be doing differently?
2. What will you be doing more or less of?
3. How will you be treating yourself, others, the world?
4. What will other people notice that's different about you, in the things you say and do?
5. What people, places, events, activities, challenges will you approach, start, resume or contact?

Now pick one of those answers.

How can you include this in your life now? If you are already doing it, how could you do it even better? Or pick another and think about how you could include that in your life.

Keep checking in with yourself.

Armed with your kitbag filled with all the tools you have learnt during this book; using your Observing Mind and the skills to *Drop the Struggle, Accept Being Uncomfortable, Play in the Now* and *Do What Matters*, you can change your behaviour, set a direction and take the steps towards these dreams. This will help you to lead the life you want to lead and be the performer you want to be.

As of yet, you have no idea about how amazing you could really be.

Notes

Introduction

1 Gloster, A. T., Walder, N., Levin, M. E., Twohig, M. P., & Karekla, M. (2020). The empirical status of acceptance and commitment therapy: A review of meta-analyses. *Journal of Contextual Behavioral Science, 18,* 181–192.

2 Bernier, M., Thienot, E., Codron, R., & Fournier, J. F. (2009). Mindfulness and acceptance approaches in sport performance. *Journal of Clinical Sport Psychology, 3*(4), 320–333.

3 Gardner, F. L., & Moore, Z. E. (2004). A mindfulness-acceptance-commitment-based approach to athletic performance enhancement: Theoretical considerations. *Behavior Therapy, 35*(4), 707–723.

Chapter 1

1 This quote is attributed to the great Yankees catcher and manager Yogi Berra. See for example Scott, N. (2019, March 28). The 50 greatest Yogi Berra quotes. *USA Today.* https://ftw.usatoday.com/2019/03/the-50-greatest-yogi-berra-quotes.

2 Adapted from Harris, R. (2019). *ACT made simple: An easy-to-read primer on acceptance and commitment therapy* (2nd ed.). New Harbinger Publications.

Chapter 2

1 Killingsworth, M. A., & Gilbert, D. T. (2010). A wandering mind is an unhappy mind. *Science, 330*(6006), 932–932. https://doi/10.1126/science.1192439.

2 Harris, R. (2019). *ACT made simple: An easy-to-read primer on acceptance and commitment therapy* (2nd ed.). New Harbinger Publications.

3 Adapted from the additional resources provided in Harris, R. (2019). *ACT made simple: An easy-to-read primer on acceptance and commitment therapy* (2nd ed.). New Harbinger Publications.

4 Noetel, M., Ciarrochi, J., Van Zanden, B., & Lonsdale, C. (2019). Mindfulness and acceptance approaches to sporting performance enhancement: A systematic review. *International Review of Sport and Exercise Psychology, 12*(1), 139–175.

5 Segal, R., & Leighton, S. (2016). *Positive psychology: Harnessing the power of happiness, mindfulness, and inner strength* (4th ed.). Harvard Health Publications.

6 Hof, W. (n.d.). *The journey of the iceman: Wim Hof's secret to defying science*. Wim Hof. https://www.wimhofmethod.com/.

7 Adapted from Hayes, S. C. (2019). *A liberated mind. The essential guide to ACT: Transform your thinking & find freedom from stress, anxiety, depression & addiction*. Vermilion.

8 Djokovic, N. (2014). *Serve to win: The 14-day gluten-free plan for physical and mental excellence*. Corgi.

9 Verhaeghen, P. (2021). Mindfulness as attention training: Meta-analyses on the links between attention, performance and mindfulness interventions, long-term meditation practice, and trait mindfulness. *Mindfulness, 12*, 564–581. https://Doi.org/10.1007/s12671-020-01532-1.

Chapter 3

1 An article referencing McIlroy's perspective on the situation can be found here: Parry, A. (2021, April 5). The one that got away: How McIlroy's Masters meltdown still haunts him. *National Club Golfer*. https://www.nationalclubgolfer.com/news/rory-mcilroy-masters-meltdown-2011/.

2 The original metaphor for this exercise can be found on p.20 of Harris, R. (2009). *ACT made simple: An easy-to-read primer on Acceptance and Commitment Therapy*. New Harbinger Publications.

3 Harris, R. (2019). *ACT made simple: An easy-to-read primer on Acceptance and Commitment Therapy* (2nd ed.). New Harbinger Publications.

4 Tichener's original exercise used lemons as we do. Other practitioners substitute other reaction provoking items such as pickle or milk. See Tichener, E. B. (1916). *A beginner's psychology*. Macmillan.

5 Hayes, S. C., Strosahl, K. D., & Wilson, K. G. (1999). *Acceptance and commitment therapy: An experiential approach to behavior change*. Guildford Press.

Chapter 4

1 Greenwood, W. (n.d.) *'Oh my God, don't lose! Will Greenwood recalls 2003 World Cup final win*. [Video]. Bein sports. https://www.youtube.com/watch?v=OcFWImsZfZg.

2 Mason, R. (2018). *Zero to hero: The Gareth Southgate story*. SJH Publishing.

3 Robert Yerkes and John Dodson first identified in 1908 that performance increases with physiological or mental arousal up to a point (see Yerkes, R. M., & Dodson, J. D. (1908). The relation of strength of stimulus to rapidity of habit-formation. *Journal of Comparative Neurology and Psychology, 18*(5), 459–482.) Stephen Williams further developed the pressure-performance curve, initially for use in business. (see Williams, S. (1994). *Managing pressure for peak performance: The positive approach to stress.* Kogan Page.)

4 Harris, R. (2019). *ACT made simple: An easy-to-read primer on acceptance and commitment therapy* (2nd ed.). New Harbinger Publications.

5 Ingle, S. (2013, July 23). Jessica Ennis-Hill back with a bang but tendon a concern for Moscow. *The Guardian.* https://www.theguardian.com/sport/2013/jul/23/jessica-ennis-hill-personal-best-javelin.

6 Yu, C., & Minsberg, T. (2021, August 8). A look at all the world records that were broken at the Tokyo Olympics. *New York Times.* https://www.nytimes.com/2021/08/08/sports/olympics/world-records-tokyo-olympics.html.

7 Leonardo, E. D., & Hen, R. (2006). Genetics of affective and anxiety disorders. *Annual Review of Psychology, 57*, 117–137. https://doi.org.10.1146/annurev.psych.57.102904.190118.

8 We use the helpful mnemonic DOTS created by psychotherapist Dr. Russ Harris. See Harris, R. (2022). *The happiness trap: How to stop struggling and start living* (2nd ed.). Robinson Publishing.

9 The Struggle Switch metaphor was first coined by Russ Harris (2008) in his book *The happiness trap: How to stop struggling and start living.* Robinson Publishing.

10 This exercise was adapted from Turrell, S. L., McCurry, C., Bell, M., & Hayes, L. L. (2018). *The mindfulness and acceptance workbook for teen anxiety: Activities to help you overcome fears and worries using acceptance and commitment therapy.* New Harbinger Publications.

11 Ruiz, F. J., & Luciano, C. (2012). Improving international level chess-players' performance with an acceptance-based protocol. *The Psychological Record, 62*, 447–461.

12 Adapted from Hayes, S. C. (2019). *A liberated mind. The essential guide to ACT: Transform your thinking & find freedom from stress, anxiety, depression & addiction.* Vermilion.

Chapter 5

1 Juggins, S., & Stainthorpe, S. (2017). *The history makers. How team GB stormed to a first ever gold in women's hockey.* Pitch Publishing.

2 Smith, P., Leeming, E., Forman, M., & Hayes, S. C. (2019). From form to function: Values and committed action strengthen mindful practices with context and direction. *Journal of Sport Psychology in Action, 10*(4), 227–234. https://doi.org.10.1080/21520704.2018.1557773.

3 Mitchell, K. (2012, September 8). Coach Ivan Lendl tells Andy Murray to have fun in the US Open final. *The Guardian*. https://www.theguardian.com/sport/2012/sep/08/ivan-lendl-andy-murray-us-open.

4 Adapted from 'The Heroes' by Rob Archer (2013) in Stoddard, J. A., & Afari, N. (2014). *The big book of ACT metaphors*. New Harbinger.

5 For an account of David Hemery's historic win read Bagchi, R. (2012, April 27). 50 stunning Olympic moments no.25: David Hemery storms to gold in Mexico. *The Guardian*. https://www.theguardian.com/sport/london-2012-olympics-blog/2012/apr/27/stunning-olympic-moments-david-hemery.

Chapter 6

1 Rohr, R. (2015, December 28). Journey to the centre. *Centre for Action and Contemplation*. https://cac.org/daily-meditations/journey-to-the-center-2015-12-28/.

2 Wood, J. V., Elaine Perunovic, W. Q., & Lee, J. W. (2009). Positive self-statements: Power for some, peril for others. *Psychological Science, 20*(7), 860–866. https://doi.org.10.1111/j.1467-9280.2009.02370.x.

3 Wood, J. V., Elaine Perunovic, W. Q., & Lee, J. W. (2009). Positive self-statements: Power for some, peril for others. *Psychological Science, 20*(7), 860–866. https://doi.org.10.1111/j.1467-9280.2009.02370.x.

4 Harris, R. (2010). *The confidence gap: From fear to freedom*. Penguin UK.

5 This defusion technique is widely used by ACT practitioners. See for example: Hayes, S. (2019). 5 effective exercises to help you stop believing your automatic unwanted thoughts. *TED*. https://ideas.ted.com/5-effective-exercises-to-help-you-stop-believing-your-unwanted-automatic-thoughts/.

6 Cooper, E. (2018, January 23). Michael Phelps opens up about his battle with depression. *Men's Health*. https://www.menshealth.com/uk/mental-strength/a758675/michael-phelps-opens-up-about-his-battle-with-depression/.

7 Finance, E. (2021, July 8). Michael Phelps on why It's 'challenging' for athletes to admit their mental health struggles. *People*. https://people.com/sports/michael-phelps-on-why-its-challenging-for-athletes-to-admit-mental-health-struggles/.

8 Sky Sports. (2022, July 11). Wimbledon: Nick Kyrgios feels like he 'belongs' and speaks about 'drunk fan' who interfered in final. https://www.skysports.com/tennis/news/32498/12649629/wimbledon-nick-kyrgios-feels-like-he-belongs-and-speaks-about-drunk-fan-who-interfered-in-final.

9 See for example Walker, S. (2019). Negative self-appraisal mediates the relationship between mindfulness and confidence among adolescent female provincial hockey players in South Africa. *South African Journal of Sports Medicine, 31*(1), 1–5. http://dx.doi.org/10.17159/2078-516x/2019/v31i1a4371; or Pineau, T. R., Glass, C. R., Kaufman, K. A., & Bernal, D. R. (2014). Self-and team-efficacy beliefs of rowers and their relation to mindfulness and flow. *Journal of Clinical Sport Psychology, 8*(2), 142–158.

10 Polk, K. L., Schoendorff, B., Webster, M., & Olaz, F. O. (2016). *The essential guide to the ACT Matrix: A step-by-step approach to using the ACT Matrix model in clinical practice.* New Harbinger Publications.

11 Adapted from Hill, D., & Sorensen, D. (2021). *ACT Daily Journal: Get unstuck and live fully with acceptance and commitment therapy.* New Harbinger Publications.

Chapter 7

1 Washif, J. A., Farooq, A., Krug, I., Pyne, D. B., Verhagen, E., Taylor, L., … Chamari, K. (2022). Training during the COVID-19 lockdown: Knowledge, beliefs, and practices of 12,526 athletes from 142 countries and six continents. *Sports Medicine, 52*(4), 933–948.

2 Aston Martin Aramco Cognizant F1 Team. (2022, July 28). Sebastian Vettel announces F1 retirement [video]. YouTube. https://www.youtube.com/watch?v=r3BgDLfRTjk

3 Adapted from Hayes, S. C. (2019). *A liberated mind. The essential guide to ACT: Transform your thinking & find freedom from stress, anxiety, depression & addiction.* Vermilion.

4 See for example Singh, M., & Sanwalka, S. (2013). *The race of my life: An autobiography.* Rupa Publications India Pvt. Limited; BBC. (2021, June 19). Milkha Singh: India's 'Flying Sikh' dies from Covid. https://www.bbc.co.uk/news/world-asia-india-57523457.

5 Fogg, B. J. (2019). *Tiny habits: The small changes that change everything.* Eamon Dolan Books.

6 Lally, P., Van Jaarsveld, C. H., Potts, H. W., & Wardle, J. (2010). How are habits formed: Modelling habit formation in the real world. *European Journal of Social Psychology, 40*(6), 998–1009.

7 Clear, J. (2018). *Atomic habits: An easy & proven way to build good habits & break bad ones.* Random House.

Chapter 8

1 Howells, K., & Lucassen, M. (2018). 'Post-Olympic blues' — The diminution of celebrity in Olympic athletes. *Psychology of Sport and Exercise, 37,* 67–78. https://doi.org/10.1016/j.psychsport.2018.04.008.

2 Palminteri, S., Khamassi, M., Joffily, M., & Coricelli, G. (2015). Contextual modulation of value signals in reward and punishment learning. *Nature Communications, 6*(1), 1–14.

3 See for example: Sarkar, M., Fletcher, D., & Brown, D. J. (2015). What doesn't kill me…: Adversity-related experiences are vital in the development of superior Olympic performance. *Journal of Science and Medicine in Sport, 18*(4), 475–479; Hardy, L., Barlow, M., Evans, L., Rees, T., Woodman, T., & Warr, C. (2017). Great British medalists: Psychosocial biographies of super-elite and elite athletes from Olympic sports. *Progress in Brain Research, 232,* 1–119: Howells, K., Sarkar, M., & Fletcher, D. (2017). Can athletes benefit from difficulty? A systematic review of growth following adversity in competitive sport. *Progress in Brain Research, 234,* 117–159.

4 Adapted from Hayes, S. C. (2019). *A liberated mind. The essential guide to ACT: Transform your thinking & find freedom from stress, anxiety, depression & addiction.* Vermilion.

5 Rose, G. (2016, September 1). Italian Grand Prix: Niki Lauda's F1 comeback drive at Monza, 40 years on. *BBC.* https://www.bbc.co.uk/sport/formula1/37243696.

6 Originally devised by Russ Harris, there are many versions of this exercise available. See for example Harris, R. (2022). *The happiness trap: How to stop struggling and start living* (2nd ed.). Robinson Publications.

7 See these sources for the storyL King, S. (2018, December 7). Free diving world record holder Sofia Gomez Uribe on her love and the danger of The Big Blue. *9 News.* https://www.9news.com.au/national/sofia-gomez-uribe-free-diving -personal-best/eb06db48-7ee6-4fcf-a4b1-3603c7720ca1; Deeper Blue. (2020, October 13). Colombian freediving superstar Sofia Gomez on rediscovering her love of competition, and David Attenborough's 'a life on our planet' documentary. https://podcast.deeperblue.com/colombian-freediving-superstar-sofia-gomez-on -rediscovering-her-love-of-competition-and-david-attenboroughs-a-life-on-our -planet-documentary; Whelan, S. (2022, July 29). Vertical blue 2022: Everything you need to know. *Deeper Blue.* https://www.deeperblue.com/vertical-blue-2022 -everything-you-need-to-know/.

8 Adapted from Polk, K. L., Schoendorff, B., Webster, M., & Olaz, F. O. (2016). *The essential guide to the ACT Matrix: A step-by-step approach to using the ACT Matrix model in clinical practice.* New Harbinger Publications and from Hayes, S. C. (2019). *A liberated mind. The essential guide to ACT: Transform your thinking & find freedom from stress, anxiety, depression & addiction.* Vermilion.

Chapter 9

1 The idea of having a Choice Point was introduced in Ciarrochi, J., Kashdan, T. B., & Harris, R. (2013). *The foundations of flourishing.* New Harbinger Publications, Inc.

2 Nystrom, M. (2019, January 14). Now what? 6 pro athletes share what happened after achieving their dream. *Polar.* https://www.polar.com/blog/6-pro-athletes-after -achieving-dream/.

Index

Acceptance 7, 61–64, 119
Anchors 28
Andy Murray 73
Anxiety 9–10, 29, 53–57, 64–66, 96–100, 123–129, 141, 150
Attention 16–17, 24–36, 42–45, 97–102, 108, 120, 126, 144
Avoidance 54–58, 100, 114, 137–142

Beach ball 17
Brain 11–12, 20, 38, 56, 70, 96, 109, 123
British women's hockey team 72
Butterflies 57

Choice point 138–145
Comfort zone 4, 9, 53–61, 72, 83, 99
Commitment 74, 82, 113, 139
Confidence 2, 66, 81–85, 89–103, 129–132

David Hemery 78
Defusion 41–44, 95
Direction 5–8, 10, 31–35, 50, 69–98, 103–109, 123, 131–134, 136, 151
Distraction 24, 34, 42, 59–62
Dream 9–10, 54, 68–74, 79–81, 87–88, 108, 124, 132, 135–138, 145, 149–151
Drop anchor 129–130, 135
Doubt 37–38, 56, 91–96, 99–102, 111, 120, 140

Energy 9, 34, 41, 46–49, 52, 57–64, 67–72, 89, 97, 103–117, 121, 131, 137, 148
Environment 56, 113, 120

Failure 7, 17, 45–46, 54–55, 72, 83, 88, 121, 123–133
Focus 6–7, 13, 23–36, 46–48, 55, 66, 72, 80, 94–96, 97–99, 108, 111, 116, 120–124, 127, 130–135

Gareth Southgate 53
Goals 15, 42, 70–73, 77–84, 101–104, 108–109, 113, 119, 138, 145
Grounding 28

Habits 109–114, 121
High performance 7, 49, 64, 71, 88, 98, 116, 123–124

Injury 55, 59, 105, 116, 123, 129–131
Ivan Lendl 73

Jessica Ennis-Hill 55

Kitbag 4, 10, 20, 35, 50, 62, 66–67, 84–88, 101–102, 114, 121, 134–138, 142–148, 151
Krista Pärmäkoski 149

Meaning and purpose 67
Michael Phelps 96
Milkha Singh 107–108
Mindful 21–36, 87, 98–102, 119, 137, 143–148
Motivation 5, 13, 56–57, 81–88, 102–116, 121, 132, 143, 149

Nelson Mandela 92
Nerves 6, 11, 23, 53–58, 64–66, 91–94
Nick Kyrgios 98
Niki Lauda 127
Noticing 16–20, 26–30, 33, 47, 66, 93–97, 101, 118–119, 126, 132, 144

Observing mind 12–21, 26, 35–36,
40–43, 47, 85–88, 102, 114, 124, 134,
142, 148
Olympians 123
Opting out 59, 131

Panic 53–56, 61
Potential 1, 6, 9, 35, 64–66, 84–85, 110,
114, 134, 142–143, 150
Pressure performance curve 53–55

Response to pressure 51–58, 67
Reason-giving 13, 47, 141
Roger Federer 93
Roy McIlroy 37

Sebastian Vettel 105
Selection 74, 123, 129
Self-compassion 145–147

Self-esteem 89–90, 124
Sensations 19–20, 26–33, 52, 63–64, 119
Setbacks 85–88, 121–139
Sofía Gómez Uribe 131
Sport roadmap 67, 78–84, 108
Stretch zone 53–56, 61, 67
Stuck loop 25, 99–101
Substances 59

Urges 20, 58, 63, 116–120
Usain Bolt 92, 139

Values 71–84, 103–108, 115, 120,
132–139, 148–150

Will Greenwood 52
Wim Hof 29

Yellowtail moth 128–129, 135

Milton Keynes UK
Ingram Content Group UK Ltd
UKHW022320020424
440481UK00015B/688

9 781914 110269